Focus!

Drop the Law of Attraction. Slay Your Goals.

The PROVEN guide to huge success, a powerful attitude and profound love.

By David Essel, M.S.

#1 Best-Selling Author, Counselor, Master Life and
Business Coach, Inspirational Speaker

Front cover photo by Lisa Belcher
Back cover photo by Terry Essel
Formatting by Leigh (Bella) St John

Copyright © 2018 David Essel

www.DavidEssel.com

Foreword

"I remember the first time I had David Essel on my SiriusXM show. I love the power of positive thinking, so I was very curious as to what this guy was going to talk about when he was my guest with his book "Positive thinking will never change your life... But this book will! The myth of positive thinking, the reality of success."

Was I skeptical? Well let's just say intrigued. So he comes onto the show and I decided to give him a few minutes to explain why he believes that positive thinking is a myth. Four minutes later? I was absolutely sold.

I actually stopped the show for second, turned to my listeners, and said "you've got to listen to what this man is saying he's the real deal. He knows what he's talking about."

And it's true. Why is he a regular returning guest to my show? Because David has the experience, knowledge, and believe it or not, such a positive attitude, and his energy is infectious.

With his new book, "Focus! The PROVEN guide to huge success, a great attitude and profound love.", I find the same infectious attitude, powerful information, that will help you get back on track to accomplish everything you could want in life.

With "Focus", David goes deeply into the concept of profound love. He discusses something he created years ago that we've discussed several times on my show "the love scale, 1 to 10".

I'm excited to endorse his new book, just as excited as I was to endorse his last one, and which I said and still believe to this day " David Essel is the new leader of the positive thinking movement."

May your life be enriched in attitude, success and love through this book."

Love,

Jenny McCarthy
Radio host, actress, best-selling author.

False: **"We become what we think about all day long."** *Buddha*

Truth: **"We become what we do all day long."** *David Essel*

"David Essel's destiny is to help you become more alive in every area of your life."
~ Dr. Wayne W. Dyer

"David is the radiant soul of radio. He is brilliant, insightful and easy to listen to. David makes a real difference in his listeners' lives."
~ Mark Victor Hansen, Chicken Soup for the Soul

Table of Contents

Dedication

This book is dedicated to my brother Terry,
who has been a source of strength in my life in many, many
ways.

The paths we choose to walk are often filled
with challenges unforeseen, and we all need companions
like my brother
who will walk through those challenges
with us.

Terry has been that Companion
for me, many times over,
and to many other people in this world, as well. "The Kid",
as I call him,
is a rock in my life.

I love you, bro,

David

Action is the foundational key to all success.

Pablo Picasso

Introduction

I have come to realize that we get out of life what we focus our thoughts on, and just as importantly, what we focus our actions on, on a daily basis. Over the years many people have put the emphasis for our success on the power of thought, from books to DVDs and movies. So what we see today in regards to goal achievement and goal setting is about focusing our thoughts. While this is incredibly important, what you are going to find out in this book, and what I think separates this book from so many other products on personal growth and motivation, is that we are going to look not just at what our mind is doing, but what our actions are doing, or not doing, on a daily basis as well.

When I look at my life 37 years ago, I can tell you that I fell victim as well to all of the hype and hoopla around the teaching that says if we just focus our mind in a certain way, life will dramatically change. For years, I even taught this theory about "focusing our mind, focusing our mind, focusing our mind," but what happened in my life, and what has happened to millions and millions of other people, is that this concept can only get us so far. Eventually the mind is either going to retreat into old behaviors and old belief systems, because it actually does not believe it when we say that, "I own seven homes around the world today," when in actuality, we are renting a mobile home. There is nothing wrong with renting a mobile home, but I think you get the picture. This book is going to offer a different look at focus. The mind is important, but there is much, much more that we are going to cover in regards to this and the overall goal of achieving more in life.

The other thing that is going to separate this book from many other concepts regarding success is that we are going to focus on a simple formula, an extremely unique goal achievement system, that if followed, you will be finally able to exceed your own expectations in every area of life. I am so excited to introduce this system via this book to the world. We have been working with this success concept since 1996, and now, after years of changing thousands of people's lives from all over the world through our 1-on-1 sessions and private class settings, we are sharing this success secret now, so that the power of this system can help millions of more people to focus and exceed their own expectations in life.

If you apply the principles in this book, you will experience huge success, a great attitude and create profound love. You will see your life change, and then as importantly, you will start to see the lives of those around you shift as well. The world will change when you apply these principles. Now some people, they might say, "Wow! This guy is an egomaniac. He is telling me that if I follow the program in this book, that I myself can change the world." And the answer is, absolutely yes. You see, we have condensed some of the most powerful teachings since the beginning of time into this book to help you focus. There is no need to recreate wheels. There is no need to go out and continue to search and look, because in our searching and in our looking we often overlook one major tenet to success, and that is the focus of our daily actions. We are going to deeply explore the significance of our daily actions in this book. At the end of this book, I only want one thing for you: I want you to see that you hold the power in your own life, and that by applying certain techniques in a specific way, you will be able to exceed your own expectations. I have seen it happen with thousands of people that we have worked with. I know it can happen with you. Let's get ready to rock, and find out just how powerful the concept of focus is in becoming more successful in life.

Focus! Chapter 1:
Why This Book and Why Now?

"You are worthy of every goal you desire."

Let me go back in time. For the past 37 years, I have had the opportunity to practice these principles that we are writing about, and I have also had the opportunity to practice many other principles; some successful, some not. I have hit great setbacks in life. Like many of you reading this book, I thought that I was highly focused and on a path of success, only to have something happen with my health, finances, relationships, or my spiritual path, that knocked me off track.

In these 37 years, I have had a chance to interview some of the most amazing minds in this world. I mean incredible brains, people who are highly successful: in the world of sports, business, personal growth, and in the world of spirituality. Everyone from Deepak Chopra, to Suze Orman, to Lama Surya Das, an amazing spiritual leader, to Father Ron, from the Hanley Center. I have had a chance to interact with people like Maharishi Mahesh Yogi, whom I will tell you an amazing story about later, and authors like JJ Virgin, Wayne Dyer and the singers Kenny Loggins and Meatloaf. All of these people, have something in common with other highly successful individuals, like Harv Eker, the financial teacher, and that "something in common" is what you will find out in this book. They are all highly focused people.

This book, is actually a follow-up to our number one bestseller "Positive thinking will never change your life… But this book will! The myth of positive thinking the reality of success." The response to that book, obviously, was off the charts. And now we get to push the boundaries a little bit further with our new book.

The major difference between this book, and our last one, is that we're going to offer you a step-by-step guideline on how to create the most incredible life you could ever imagine. Daily steps. Action steps. We're going to challenge the whole concept of affirmations, and give you the reality of success when it comes to the world of thinking.

And we're going to give you a step-by-step approach on how to create an action plan, that might actually surprise you. This program "The one thing theory" TM, was created in 1996 and to this very day I have found nothing that can compare to the power of this program in helping you to create a daily and weekly action program to achieve whatever it is you want in life.

As you follow the guidelines exactly as we present them in this book, I promise you will thrive. Your passion for life will either return or be heightened. The journey will become clear, the adventure of achieving goals will be realized.

But the path may not be easy. Any huge goal that you have right now will require a huge effort. We need to focus to win.

I'll share stories of people who through the focused approach to living diagnosed in this book accomplished massive goals. Like Evelyn, who lost 245 pounds to become a bodybuilder in her 50s!

Or Thomas, who after 30 years of addictions to opiates and alcohol not only got sober, but turned his marriage into something so beautiful for him and his wife.

And I'll share a story of how I used the very principles in this book to forgive a former lover, who I told myself I could never forgive, and reclaim a new attitude about her that I thought would never be possible.

But wait, there is so much more to the story. As the author of this book, and the creator of this powerful program on focus, I want to share with you the multiple ways I have used this technique over the years to great benefit in my personal and professional life. You might see yourself in one of these scenarios as well.

Probably like you, I've struggled over and over and over again in life. But by following the system you are about to read, I've been able to accomplish the following:

Through focus I became sober after 25 years of struggling with cocaine and alcohol.

Through focus I shattered my own codependency in romantic relationships after struggling in this arena for over 30 years.

Through focus, this book that you're holding right now, my tenth book, two of them have already become number one bestsellers, even though I do not have any background in literature, creative writing or the world of communication.

By following the techniques that I am putting in this book , I became a top motivational radio talk-show host with my own syndicated show for 27 years, even though I have no background in broadcast journalism.

Through focus I've been able to help raise several children, none of my own, over the past 40 years with a combination of extreme patience, love and discipline.

Through focus I've been able to radically change my body and at 61 years of age, may have the opportunity soon to be on another cover of a fitness magazine. It was exactly 30 years ago when I was selected for the cover of

Men's Fitness magazine. Age, has no role in what you want to create in your life, if you use the power of focus.

And going back more than 40 years ago, through the power of focus I was able to make the Syracuse University junior varsity basketball team as a walk on. How? It wasn't my great athletic ability, I laugh as I write this, but rather deciding to become a defensive expert, which first got the attention of the coaches.

Over the years, with great dedication, I had learned how to "shut down" any player that I was guarding. After that I focused my attention on shooting, and actually lead the Syracuse University junior varsity basketball team in free-throw percentage for two years in a row averaging 83% from the line.

And even though I'm short, somewhat slow, and an average leaper, I was offered a walk on position on the Syracuse University varsity basketball team after my sophomore year. How did all this happen? It was focus, focus and more focus on what I was doing on a daily basis in the world of sports, not just what I was thinking.

And let me make this point so perfectly clear, the above achievements that I have seen in my life have been created because of my own dedication, perseverance and persistence. But I don't want to fool anyone. I've also searched from when I was a little kid to today, and surrounded myself with people that were better, smarter and more successful than I am.

I learned early on what I'm teaching you right now in this book, that we must surrender 110% to someone else's program, if we don't have what we want in our world today regarding our bodies, money, relationships and our attitude.

I share these above stories not to impress you, but to show

you that someone like myself who has no huge genetic gifts, no incredible intellectual gifts, that through extreme focus and dedication can accomplish massive goals in life.

And this is what I want for you. I want you to know that regardless of where you are right now, or how long you've been struggling with procrastination and lack of focus, that you can do what I have done and even better! You, have the power with this program to radically turn your life around. To live the life you desire. To stop dreaming and to start living right now. That, is what I want for you.

You'll experience huge success in the one area of life that is currently holding you back. Your attitude will slowly undergo a massive metamorphosis, until you realize you are truly unstoppable.

And profound love, with your current partner or a new one will appear, filling your heart with peace, excitement and contentment.

Focus equals discipline. Determination. Focus equals success. Inner peace. Focus increases our self-esteem and self-confidence.

When our last book came out exposing the myth of positive thinking, we received one of the most powerful endorsements that I could've ever hoped to receive. (Now, I'm still a huge fan of positive thinking when done correctly, not just in the way that it's currently taught today.)

This is the story of my friend, super celebrity Jenny McCarthy. Jenny tells a part of it in her foreword in this book that you've already read. But the full story is worth repeating now.

My publicist TJ Tauriello was scanning the country, booking us on a weekly basis on radio and TV shows. Within just a few months of working with me, he excitedly texted me one day and said that we had just been booked with Jenny McCarthy.

Now I have always loved Jenny McCarthy. Yes, from her Playboy magazine days, to her cohosting on TV, to her movies and now everything she's doing including her radio show on Sirius XM satellite radio.

So, to find out I was going to be a guest on her show put me over-the-top. I couldn't wait. I was thrilled, beyond belief.

In talking to one of her producers before the show, the producer told me that Jenny was a huge fan of positive thinking, and that it was going to be an excellent and interesting interview.

I started to think to myself, I really hope Jenny has an open mind, because my book is about the myth of positive thinking, and the reality of success. I knew if I had just a few minutes to explain the concept, that she would understand it, she may not agree with it, but I knew she would understand it.

And then the surprise of my life happened. Jenny welcomes me to the show, introduces me as a guy that's written a book about the myth of positive thinking, and our energies collided in the most positive of ways! Oh, my Lord the first two minutes of the show I thought I was talking to myself. It was fantastic. Her high-energy, incredible wit, was a perfect match for me and my passion for life.

After a few minutes of a brief introduction, she says "David, go ahead and give us the premise of your book. You know I'm a huge fan of positive thinking, and I'm dying to hear what you have to say."

And with that, I was off to the races. In about three minutes I had diagrammed my complete breakdown of how some books that tell us we can "achieve whatever we believe", was not true. And I started giving fact after fact after fact to prove the point.

After 3 to 4 minutes I got the surprise of my life, as Jenny stops the show and says this. "I want everyone to listen to this man David Essel... He is the real deal. He knows what he's talking about. There are a lot of illusions out there that maybe we all have bought into, but let's follow his advice from here on out."

I was in heaven. The rest of the interview, I was walking on cloud nine. Jenny McCarthy, a huge fan of positive thinking, immediately grasped what my entire book was all about in just a 3 to 4-minute explanation.

Several weeks later to add to the excitement and surprise, TJ sends me this endorsement that we got from Jenny in an email, "David Essel is The new leader of the positive thinking movement."

How much better could it get? I was invited back on her show four more times within 12 months. And every time I'm on the show Jenny and I click like peanut butter and jelly. We have the same passion, the same wit, the same drive, the same energy... And she's always been so open about her own life, successes, and everything that has brought her to where she is today.

And then just when I thought it couldn't get any better, Jenny agreed to write the foreword to this book. All of us in the world of positive thinking say that we need to validate our own belief systems, and not wait for the outside world to validate them for us, but Jenny McCarthy's endorsement means the world to me.

Law of Attraction?

When we discuss the power of focus, we must also slow down and examine one of the most popular theories in the world of success that might be actually holding you back in life. Yes, actually holding you back from accomplishing the most important goals that you desire right now.

And it might surprise you to know that this popular theory that I'm referring to, is called the famous law of attraction. The law of attraction has been around since the beginning of time, but the popularity of this program went through the roof around 2007 and unfortunately is still talked about today as one of the most important keys to long-term success.

It is not true. It never truly has been the key to success and never will be. As a matter of fact 80% of the current teachings of the law of attraction are fantasy, falsehoods, and they may actually hold more people back from accomplishing their goals then help them.

So, do you want to keep dreaming? Or you or are you really ready to start living? Living the dreams you've always had?

For many people reading this right now, I am stomping on sacred ground here with this statement, but follow me and I can prove that what I'm saying and have been teaching since 1996 is the truth about success. No fantasy, no fantastical thinking, simply the truth.

And, there is no one more qualified today than myself to expose the myth of the teachings that surround us, like the law of attraction. And do you know why this is true? Because from 1980 until 1996 that's sixteen straight years, I used to teach this philosophy. It never worked the way we said it would back then, and it still doesn't today.

And, for my role in promoting a program and philosophy that does not work, I am sorry. When I used to travel the world during those years, I proclaimed onstage comments like "whatever you believe you can achieve", and "whatever you positively focus your thoughts on you'll automatically attract this into your life."

Oh my Lord was I ever wrong. I so wish this stuff worked, but huge success, a great attitude and profound love will never come to us just because we believe they will.

Then in 1996, through my interview with Maharishi Mahesh Yogi, the founder of transcendental meditation, all of this positive thinking, positive affirmation and "attracting huge success through your thoughts", was blown out of the water for me.

During this interview, he showed me that not one of my affirmations that I had been teaching around the world for 16 years had ever come true in my life via my thoughts! Again, I was blown away, my world actually seemed to crash down on that very day. But, I've come to realize since then that he gave me a gift, the gift of reality.

You see, I've never met anyone who teaches these law of attraction principles that can honestly say they've worked for them either. Isn't that interesting?

As a matter of fact, do you know anyone who's become a millionaire via their thoughts alone? Or who has achieved a phenomenal body because they built a vision board with pictures of beautiful physiques on them, and somehow their body just attracted this into their lives?

By now, you've heard the ridiculous claims about how, "if you imagine checks in the mail, they must come to you." Really? Are you serious?

Or how about, "if you put a picture of a $1 million house on a vision board and tuck that board in a storage facility that a few years down the road, without doing any work, you'll be living in that home."

Seriously? And yes, I apologize, I used to teach this nonsense. In 38 years now working full-time in the world of personal growth, I've never interviewed even one person, who said huge success came to them in this way.

As Susan Powter so perfectly put it years ago, "stop the insanity now!"

Through the power of focus, what we are saying right now is that it's time for a huge reality check. Your thoughts do not become materialistic things, like money or a new home, or a new car on their own. If something like this did happen, let's say you imagined winning the lottery, and you do the very next day, that's called a miracle. Plain and simple. A miracle.

I will confidently tell you this. 80% of the law of attraction, the way it is ridiculously promoted today, is a lie. A flat out lie. 20% of it is true. For instance, if you want to become wealthy and you start hanging around with wealthy people, and do exactly what these wealthy people do every day, you have an edge on everyone else and you might just become wealthy. But there's not even a guarantee if you follow everything a wealthy person does, that you will become wealthy as well.

Let me take this one step further. Recently a famous law of attraction teacher posted on my Facebook wall this advertisement: "Would you like to learn how to make $100,000 in a weekend through the law of attraction? Are you tired of working hard and not making the money that you want? Join my webinar and learn how to use the power of your mind alone, with the law of attraction, to become wealthy."

Ridiculous. And worse than that, this type of teaching is downright dangerous. She is preying on people that are struggling financially and taking advantage of them by charging for a webinar that promises the impossible. I immediately deleted her post.

That is just the tip of the iceberg. These type of advertisements are going on via all sorts of social media on a daily basis. Several months ago I received an email from another very famous law of attraction teacher promising instant weight loss through the power of the mind.

This is what her email said.

"Are you stuck at a weight and frustrated? Have you tried every diet in the world and still feel ashamed of how you look?

The key to long-term weight loss is to learn how to use the law of attraction to get the body you've always wanted. No more exercise needed. No more recording what you've been eating. No more work needed to get the body you desire! Join my weekend workshop today."

I know that this insanity must stop so that we can all create a life of joy, success and deep love. I have no interest in mentioning any names in this book, but please, buyer beware. Common sense. Let's start to use some logical thinking, as we go after the most important goals that we have in our lives right now.

While some people may balk at my premise about this fantastical thinking stuff, I am not the only professional with 38 years of experience in the world of personal growth who feels the same way I do.

My friend, Dr. Eldon Taylor, one of the foremost experts in the world regarding the power of the mind, wrote this as part of his foreword to my number one best selling book, "Positive Thinking Will Never Change Your Life ...But this book will!"

"Unfortunately, a common belief today arises from a bestselling book that promises fortune if you but only magnetize your thoughts with what you want. You might expect it to be a best seller when you think about it, for it basically tells us we don't need to work hard for anything—we can just visualize it. Let me flesh that out a little. The so-called "Secret" suggests that our thinking is like a giant magnet that attracts kind, and thus the over used and immature notion that there is this thing called the law of attraction that is thought based alone. Thank God that's not so, or many of us might have experienced some truly unpleasant results from our passing moments of fatigue, frustration, anger and the like! Still, there are those adamant believers of this nonsense who insist that everything that happens to us is brought to us because we have "magnetized" it with our thoughts.

This is so ridiculous that I once even heard a popular guru of the law of attraction state that another teacher of the law of attraction, one who had organized a sweat lodge that led to the deaths of two followers, had attracted this because of his thinking. How can any intelligent and sensible human being look at a victim of rape, incest, or any other violent crime; and/or the cancer or terminal patient, and insist that they attracted their situation due to their magnetic thoughts?

As you read David's bold new work you will discover exactly why this is not only nonsense, but also very dangerous nonsense at that! David is a positive thinker who has empowered the lives of many through his teachings. In this book he explains how important your expectation, perception and life beliefs are. He will share with you in the pages that follow just how you can actualize your ambitions. This powerful book urges action and renounces the idea that success can simply be magnetized using incense, a vision board, affirmations and so forth.

We live in a world of action. We know time only as a result of action. Before this there was that, and after this there will be—and on and on it goes. This book is all about action—the action it takes to realize your personal best in everything you do. With that come the rewards you are seeking, whatever they might be. You will learn how to succeed whether it's fame and fortune or love and joy."

Enjoy the journey and here's to your very best in everything you do!

Eldon Taylor, Ph.D., FAPANY Times Bestselling Author of "Choices and Illusions"

I recently was a guest expert on an online summit with Julie Cairnes from Australia. During this interview, Julie asked me about following our intuition when trying to create huge success in life. She agrees with me that all the hoopla around philosophies like the law of attraction can easily be more harmful than helpful. This is what I told her audience regarding following our intuition.

"Julie, for those who are truly tuned in to their own intuition, the law of attraction, especially the fantastical theories all of these teachers are promoting today, would never gain a foothold in their minds at all.

Those with a powerful connection to their own intuition would simply say "What? Attracting checks in the mail via our thoughts with no effort? That's simply too good to be true. I don't buy it."

But many of us, want this to be true. We want to believe that success can somehow be effortless, so we swallow these teachings hook, line and sinker. It's sad, but true."

Julie followed up with me after the summit and shared that so many of her listeners loved our interview and I know they are now going to be moving away from "these fantastical teachings", and into the realistic program that we are describing right now in our book.

Here is a bold statement that I want you to consider: "The teachings of the current law of attraction promoted by so many famous teachers can become more poisonous and hurtful to your success than helpful."

Let me explain. If you try to think your way sober, or think your way out of huge debt, or high blood pressure, or an affair in your marriage, without wanting to do the work necessary to turn your life around, you are digging a dangerously deep hole that you may never get yourself out of. This, seriously concerns me.

A number of years ago I worked with a client who had struggled with alcohol for as long as they could remember. I worked with this person multiple days a week for several months, and we were starting to see a breakthrough in the amount of alcohol they consumed on a daily basis as well as their attitude about finally, truly wanting to change. They had come to the realization, that getting sober, living a life without alcohol at all, would be the smartest move for their physical health and their family.

And then one day they came in, and shared that they had been at a weekend retreat with a popular spiritual teacher who had given them some terrible advice.

When my client shared with the teacher this struggle with alcohol that they had had for number of years, the teacher smiled and looked directly into my client's eyes and said "if God wants you to be sober, you will become sober. But there's no need to struggle, or to fight it at all. Let go of all of your shame and guilt, and just realize that God is in control. Let him attract the level of sobriety that he wants for you, but for now, when you drink just enjoy it. Start to think about becoming sober, and allow it to happen if it supposed to."

I could not believe what I was hearing. How dangerous is that message for an alcoholic to hear? Allow your thoughts, and God's will, to decide if you're going to get sober? Immediately what came to mind is "That's just fantastic. Let's have every alcoholic in the world driving on our streets, free of shame and guilt, and allowing God to get them sober if God wants them sober. Let's just teach every alcoholic, to put out some healthy thoughts regarding alcohol, and if they're supposed to get sober by attracting it to them they somehow will."

I wish the story I just told you was not true. It saddens my heart, that along with the law of attraction, there are other insane teachings and teachers out there today in the world of personal growth and spirituality, that are actually destroying an individual's chance of leading a happy, healthy and productive life. Please, do not fall victim to these ridiculous teachings.

Or how about my friend Ray Higdon, and the story that he shared in my number one best-selling book on positive thinking?

Ray was down to his last dollar, a single dad with two children to support, and just found out that he would be losing his home. He contacted me and asked if we could meet for lunch, and if I could give him any advice of how to pull himself out of his current financial situation.

I loved his energy, and I knew that if he found the right product to promote and or sell, he would become a rockstar with his money once again.

After leaving our meeting, he was introduced to the law of attraction, affirmations and vision boards. He was desperate, and started using these positive thinking philosophies to try to attract money, money he desperately needed into his life. The end result of following these teachings? Absolutely zero. Nothing. Nada. No money was coming into his bank accounts via the power of his thoughts.

So he did the very next step that a logical person would do, if they weren't highly influenced by popular teachings of our day that simply don't work.

Ray went out, and found a network marketing product he absolutely loved, and started going after 20 rejections a day. Let me repeat that. He started calling upon people, meeting people, and his goal was to get 20 no's a day. He realized, that if he got 20 rejections a day, that overtime he would begin to start getting people to say yes.

Where his initial attempts to follow the law of attraction had failed, his hard, persistent and dedicated work began to pay off. Within several years he was earning over $1 million a year, and currently, he has that up to over $1 million a month.

And how do you do that? Focus. Focus. Focus. He was willing to face rejection, to do the hard work, in order to be successful in life. Exactly what we have been teaching since 1996, the same philosophy you will be reading throughout the rest of this book. Success can be yours if you're willing to do the work.

Let's stop dreaming, and start really living today.

So you might ask, why is the law of attraction still so popular today even though it doesn't work? Well, there are actually two very common-sense answers for this:

One. Our desire for instant gratification combined with our desire to get the most out of life with minimal effort. Regardless if you want to admit it or not, most of us want everything right now. You send a text, you expect an instant reply. You push the remote control on your television, and you expect instant sports, or entertainment, or whatever your television viewing interests might be.

We are flooded with the opportunity for instant gratification in every area of our life, and most of us want it with minimal effort, if any effort at all. The law of attraction taps into these two desires, and creates this falsehood that says you can have the body, the money, the car, the lover or the house you want if you only learn how to attune your thoughts to thoughts of success. I wish it were true, but it simply is not.

Two. Mass consciousness. Anytime there are huge numbers of people, that are promoting a specific philosophy, the average individual, meaning you and me, can easily get swept up into this mass consciousness whether it's good for us, healthy, true or not. It happened with Hitler. It's happened with products sold via infomercials like the "thigh master", that promote incredible changes to your body if you only put this little spring like contraption between your legs. Because so many people started to purchase this product, mass consciousness took over and if you look in your closet, you might have one that has collected both clothes and dust for years upon years now.

Also, a part of mass consciousness, is when radio hosts, celebrities and or television hosts start to promote something that may not be true or valid. It's very difficult to follow our own commonsense as well as our own intuitive voice that says, "this is simply too good to be true." So, we fall victim to following the leaders in society, regardless if they are accurate or inaccurate in what they are promoting.

But as I write this book, millions of people are finally waking up to the myth of these philosophies and the reality of success, and this book will help you to shatter the illusion's that you might have bought into and create the huge success, powerful attitude and profound love that you desire and deserve.

Here is something that you might find interesting as well. The law of attraction is much more accurate when it comes to attracting negativity and negative thoughts then positive thoughts and end results. The law of attraction is one of the main reasons why we hold onto terrible habits instead of doing what it takes to become successful in life. Let me explain.

Have you ever noticed that negative thoughts and habits, or patterns, seem to multiply without effort? And yet, when we start to think about positive thoughts and habits, that they take so much work before they become a part of our lives?

When I work with clients who are struggling with anxiety, depression, money worries or the recent health report from their doctor that says there's an issue that needs immediate attention, the negative thoughts come and begin to spiral out of control. Without even thinking, every hour upon every day becomes filled with worry, anxiety and negativity. It is effortless over a short 24 hour period of time to continue to create more anxiety with our thoughts then it is to create patterns of positive thoughts. Does that make sense?

And it's the same thing with negative habits like emotional eating, or arguing with your partner or spending more than we should. It is so easy, via this part of the law of attraction, to create a mountain out of a mole hill regarding negative thoughts and or negative habits then it is to turn those thoughts and habits around to become more positive ones.

I jokingly tell some of my clients when they are talking about the law of attraction, that I have never had a client come in and say "David I don't know what's going on. I started to think a positive thought early this morning, and I can't get it out of my mind. Or David remember two weeks ago when I couldn't get myself to go into the gym to start exercising, I can't tear myself out of the gym now." I wish the law of attraction was so powerful that these things above would happen, but again, the only way I've seen people radically turn their life around so their thoughts are mainly positive, or their actions are mainly positive, is through hard, disciplined work. But after time, the good news is that the daily hard and disciplined work will simply become who you are. And this, is awesome.

Through the action steps in this book, we will show you how to deal with the easily magnified negative thoughts and behaviors, and finally turn them around so that you're living the life you desire.

So that leads us to what the true path to success actually looks like, or we could even say if we wanted to, the new accurate law of attraction, would look like this:

Number one. Pick only one major goal to go after at a time. This will attract the concept of focus into your life.

Number two. Do the steps today that you would rather not do in order to lose the weight, make the money, become a better partner and or parent etc. This will attract the concept of discipline into your life.

Number three. Hire an accountability partner, professional, to hold your feet to the fire, to make sure you do the steps on a daily basis you'd rather not do. This will attract the concept of humility, vulnerability and the power of surrendering to someone else's program. And this my friends, will guarantee your success in life.

Stop dreaming. Start living. Now.

Let's take a look at a few different people, some you may have heard of, others maybe not, who attracted great success into their lives by living the program that we are writing about right here, that entails incredible focus.

Number one. Christopher Columbus. He surely didn't attract the success that he created in life in searching for a new land, by visualizing or using positive affirmations. He took a huge physical and mental risk that not everyone believed in; and the rest is history.

Number two. NFL punter, Marquette King with the Oakland Raiders. I had a chance to interview Marquette King and he is one of the most humble, real, individuals that I've been blessed to talk to. He did not become an NFL punter, because of the power of affirmations or visualization either. But through consistent, hard work.

Number three. Celebrity Jenny McCarthy. Here again, when I've been on Jenny's show numerous times, she will share with me her road to success, how she had to do in many cases what she would rather not have done regarding auditions, travel and more. And yet today, her success is based on her willingness to use her God-given talents and to work her butt off.

Number four. My personal physician, Paul Tritel Concierge Medicine, LLC. Paul didn't visualize his way through medical school, nor through the power of thoughts did he create his own incredibly successful concierge service as a physician. No, Paul did what he had to do regarding risk taking, education, student loans and more to become the phenomenal physician he is today.

Number five. Bodybuilding champion Rich Gaspari. I've interviewed Rich as well several times on my radio shows, and he would laugh today if he had seen any of the law of attraction teachers who are proclaiming you can attract a great body via your thoughts. Rich, and every other bodybuilder I know, understands the importance of discipline, sacrifice and more if you want to be the best in the field of bodybuilding like Rich has been.

It's time to stop dreaming and start living right now.

As you can tell from 1996 until today my philosophies about how to accomplish real success in life have changed dramatically. And, at the same time, the one thing that has never changed is my powerful and positive attitude in life.

But, I work at that as well daily. Every morning I spend the first hour immersed in gratitude, journaling, meditation and prayer. I believe with all my heart that this is an essential part of life to focus on if we want long lasting success. I love positive thinking, and I want you to embrace it as well. Fill your mind, especially in the morning, with positive thoughts, quotes, and stories to get you inspired for the day.

80% of my success, and yours too, will be based on our ability to take action steps on a daily basis that may be uncomfortable. Over time, remember I need to repeat this, these uncomfortable action steps will simply become effortless, a part of who we are.

20% of your new, huge success will be due to your positive thoughts. But that's it. 20%. Unless of course a miracle occurs, and if a miracle does occur due to your thoughts alone, that is a blessing you should appreciate every day.

I remember as a kid hearing over and over and over again my parents saying, "David J, would you just do one thing at a time." You know, I laugh now thinking about that. Even into my adult life, I have been someone that has always wanted a lot of daily stimulation. To have five-hundred projects going on at the same time. Trust me, there is a positive to that, because when you have so many projects going on, you are going to be introduced to many different philosophies, teachers and types of people. You will also be introduced to a lot of success, and a lot of failure. What I have found, just like in the writing of this book, is that when the time is right, and I apply my focus, miracles happen. And I want the same to happen for you.

Focus, you see, is the key to long-lasting success. We can only juggle so many balls at a time before we figure out that living life like this is not going to work. We can only for so long say to ourselves that we are "a jack of all trades, but a master of none" until we realize that this approach might actually be hurting us in life. At some point, we have got to get focused. I know that if you really apply the principles as we are setting them out in this book, that your dreams about achieving specific levels of success in life no longer have to be just dreams, they can become your reality. You will see that you will be able to exceed your own expectations, but it will take, and I say this to you with an open heart and an open mind, it will take you doing things differently. It will take you surrendering to a new way of thinking and acting.

When I was struggling financially, I had to surrender to a

financial coach, and have her take me by the hand down her path to success. When I wanted to radically change my body, I had to surrender to someone else's way of thinking. As a matter of fact, going back twenty years ago now, I surrendered to a guy named Bill Phillips, who wrote the book," Body For Life." Even though I did not agree initially with the system that he wrote about in his book, when I wanted to radically change my body, and become part of a body sculpting contest, I had to throw out my old belief systems, and follow someone else's to get the success that I wanted. That is called focus. When I wanted to get sober in life, which I will tell you about at the end of the book, I had to throw out my beliefs of what it meant to get sober and follow someone else's program. In other words, focus right now. Focus means that if you are not getting what you want out of a certain area of life, with your mind, your body, your relationships, your career, your finances, and you truly want to see a radical shift in that one area of life, you are going to have to surrender and follow someone else's program to get what you desire. It is that simple.

So, why is now the time that this message about focus is so needed in our world today? First, we have to agree that we are highly distracted in life. Life is moving so fast.

Between all of the different technology that is available, the five thousand channels on television, the high expectations we have for our children, to not just be in soccer and do well in school, but to be in soccer, and theatre, and political clubs, and volunteer on weekends. All of a sudden, if you look around, we see harried parents driving their children to a myriad of events, and losing themselves in the process. In other words, our desire for success has gotten so out of control, that we have lost the concept of focus. We cannot even sit down at lunch with a friend without having our iPhone go off with texts and calls, and who knows what else. This time in our lives, more than ever, we need to slow down and focus. Focus on what we desire. Focus on what is meaningful in life.

Our desire for instant gratification destroys our focus, as well. We want the big hit. We want to lose the thirty pounds today. We want to make the hundred-thousand dollars now. We want to buy the homes and flip them, and become a millionaire in two years. Do you see what I am saying? We are so distracted with technology; we are so distracted with instant gratification; we have lost the concept of the power of focus. Until now. Through this book, we will bring back the power of focus, and finally get what we desire in life.

We need to slow down. We need to sit back. We need to focus, or our life is going to pass us by, and we are going to say, "Was that all it was about?" Here is the good news: You can change all of this today by getting focused.

Then watch yourself month by month exceed your own expectations.

What makes you come alive? What stirs your heart? And what are the **blocks** getting in the way of you living with passion, joy, and a feeling of being unstoppable?

Are you ready to walk through walls, into the fires of life to create exactly what you desire?

By following the message in this book, you will create huge success, a great attitude, and profound love. Guaranteed.

Chapter Review

Stop!

Now that you finished this chapter, it is very important that we slow down, and take a few minutes to answer the questions below.

Writing slows the brain down, and allows thoughts from the subconscious to come into consciousness, and this is one way we will take deep advantage of every chapter in this book.

Write. Right now. Let's keep moving towards our goals, with action steps such as these writing exercises, and not rely on our brain to create the life we desire anymore.

1) What was covered in detail, in this chapter?

_____

_____

_____

2) What was of most interest to you and why?

_____

_____

_____

3) What are 1 or 2 actions steps, relevant to the information in this chapter, that you could take right now to help you to focus more in life? Be specific, and also put the exact day and time that you will take these steps.

_____

_____

_____

Focus! Chapter 2:
What Does it Mean to be Fully Focused in Life?

"You are worthy of every goal you desire."

So, what are the benefits of a focused life? First of all, we are going to stop juggling all those plates in the air. We are going to stop spinning five thousand plates in order to try to feel successful in life. We are going to get clear. The benefit of a focused life is clarity. The benefit of a focused life is a sharp mind. We finish projects that we start, and we are disciplined role models for our friends, our coworkers, and our family. In other words, maybe for the first time in our life people will say, "My Lord, this guy, or this woman, is finishing the projects they are starting!" A huge benefit of getting focused is that we will drop the chaos and the drama. We drop the excuses. We drop the blame game on the government, on the economy, or on our genetics. We are going to drop blaming all of these outside forces, and we are going to take responsibility for moving our lives forward.

Now, some people may say, "I don't know if that is a benefit; I kind of like projecting blame out there, and saying that I am not the reason that I do not have the money I want, the body I want, the love I want, the relationship with God I want." You see, without focus, it is very easy to stay stuck in the blame game, but with focus, choosing one goal, which I will get to later on in the book, and going after it full force, we can start to see our life radically change. But it will not happen, I promise you, until we stop making excuses for the reasons that we do not have what we want in life.

Another benefit of focus is that we will be filled with confidence and integrity. Why is that? Well, think about it. When you are focused, you pick a goal that you want, one goal at a time, and you go after it, until you accomplish it. That is going to increase your confidence in life. That is going to make you feel better about yourself. It makes sense, doesn't it? Instead of saying, "I am going to do this, and do this, and do this," and at the end of twelve months, you haven't done any of it, you are going to slow down and choose one goal. You are going to attack it with a systemized approach that we will teach you in this book, and you will complete it before you start another goal. You will increase your confidence in life.

Next is your integrity. Integrity is walking your talk. Integrity is the basis of confidence. When we are constantly saying, "I am going to make this amount of money, and I am going to lose this weight, and I am going to do this, and I am going to do that," and we are just blowing smoke. People around us think, "Whatever! There he goes again; there she goes again." So, the benefit of integrity is that you will walk your talk, and you will finish your projects. People will respect you, and once again, you will become a role model to your family and friends, and most importantly to yourself. This is the beginning of the pathway to exceeding your own expectations in life. As you can imagine, it opens a doorway that many of us have never experienced throughout our entire lives.

Now, what are the challenges of living this way? What are the challenges of living a life that is fully focused? Number one is that we have got to let go of the excuses, the justifications, and the rationalizations that we use to keep us playing small in life.

So many times, people will say, "Well, you know, I would have more money in the bank, if it wasn't for the meltdown of the housing market." Or, "You know, as soon as my kids get out of the house, or as soon as my kids graduate, or as soon as my kids...." and the list goes on, and on. "If it wasn't for my genetics, I wouldn't be carrying this extra weight." Here is the truth about genetics and weight. A University of Florida study a number of years ago concluded that even though sixty-five to seventy-five percent of the United States of America is overweight or obese, only six percent of these people could use genetics as a reason for their being overweight. You see, the challenge of living a focused life is saying, "I have to walk through the resistance; I have to walk through the blocks; I have to walk through the barriers to go after my goal." "I have to drop the excuse regarding genetics and my weight and take personal responsibility for my health habits if anything is going to change."

It's like when we look back at the story of Walt Disney, who went bankrupt before he became a huge success. (Here is a link to a video I made on Walt Disney that I think you will really like: http://davidessel.com/change-your-life-course).

The person who is not focused on their end result, choosing only one major goal to work on at a time, would not have the resolve that Walt Disney had. After their first, or second, or third bankruptcy, they'd give up on their dreams. But when we are living a focused life, the opposite occurs. Challenges are going to come up. Things are going to try to get in the way of you accomplishing your goal.

Right up front, I am telling you this. I am not telling you that living a focused life is easy. I am telling you it is worth it. There will be blocks. There will be rainy weather. There will be children getting sick on the day you are supposed to start working out in the gym. There will be all kinds of blocks that are going to come up, and we have to walk through the resistance. We have to be willing to say, "I am not going to let this knock me off my course."

Now, another challenge that may arise is that our friends, our family, and our coworkers may not like the fact that you are changing. It is so true. For the 28 years that I have worked as a counselor and master life coach, and I cannot tell you how many times a couple will come in, or an individual, and declare that they are going to make a major change in life. They are going to get sober; or go back to school. They are going to start working out with a trainer in the gym. And, their friends and their partners initially are very excited.

Imagine this. A couple comes in and sits down, and says that they are looking at improving their financial future. Together we make a decision, that in order for them to accomplish the goals that they want to accomplish, that number one, they have got to start saving now, even though they don't think they can. So, we work through that hurdle; and life is good. We've got them on that pathway to success. Next, the wife decides that she has got to go back to school to get a degree in order to get a better job and move forward in life. Everyone is excited. The first couple of weeks go by; and when they come back in, all hell is breaking loose. Everyone is upset with the new goals. Why is that? Because, now that the wife is not home three nights a week until 10:00 or 10:30 at night, it is disrupting their normal routine. So, while the husband initially was really excited about his wife going back to school and their future being more secure with her job change, now it is interfering with his life. Not only does he have to make dinner nightly, but he has to take care of the kids those three nights by himself. If we are not focused, and we are standing in the wife's shoes, it is very easy to be swayed, and for her to say, "You know what, honey? You are right. This is too much on you. I am going to quit school, and we will figure out another way."

But, that is not the answer anymore. When we get focused, we say, "I know there are going to be challenges; I am not going to hide behind the façade that says, "Now that we have decided that we are going to make more money, now that we have decided we are going to lose the weight, now that we have decided we are going to forgive someone who has hurt us in the past, that it's going to be easy." Resistance, blocks, and barriers will occur; but, in our work, and by what you are reading right now, we are preparing ourselves, so that when the rationalizations and justifications to drop the goal come up, when the excuses arise, or when the going gets tough, we stay focused anyway.

Our family and friends and coworkers may think initially, I am going to repeat this, that what you are doing is great. But when it starts to affect them, they may not be in your corner. And that is okay. I have worked with many people who have made the decision to get sober, and at first their friends are all excited about them doing this, until it starts to affect the relationship. I have seen relationships break up because one partner got so focused on their recovery, and the other one tried to sabotage it. We have to make decisions for ourselves on the path to real success and realize that not everyone is going to be in our corner for the long run, and that's okay.

Left-Brain, Right-Brain

Let's look at the concept of focus as it relates to "left-brained" and "right-brained" people in life. If you're a left-brained person, "left brains" are logical. They are analytical. They are intellectual. For these types of individuals reading this book, when we get to the systems, the formulas, the action steps, and the writing exercises, you will love it. I promise you that this will excite you, because these concepts are strengths of yours.

When I have you organizing five days a week doing certain tasks on a daily basis to stay highly focused on: writing the book, losing the weight, making more money, finding your lover, or recreating a deep love relationship, …when we get to all of that systemized stuff, you are going to love it. However, when we get to some of the softer parts of life, like meditation, or lighting a candle in the morning to get focused, those things you would like to shy away from, don't shy away. Walk into the uncomfortable. Do those tasks that we recommend in this book that are not the easiest to do, because that's where success lies.

Now, what about our "right-brained" friends reading this? The "right brains" are the creative people, the spontaneous people, the "free spirits." For you, when we get to the candle lighting, or burning incense, or when we talk about following some of the practices of meditation and opening our hearts to the world, you will love it. You will immerse yourself in it. You will want to stay in that atmosphere of freedom; that atmosphere of a spiritual approach to staying focused in life. However, when we start talking about the daily structured system, the writing exercises to keep us on path, those things that demand of you to do what is not natural, you may want to shy away from these procedures. Like I mentioned above, don't. Whatever it is that you don't feel comfortable with is usually, for both the left-brained and the right-brained person, the key to success.

Isn't that interesting?

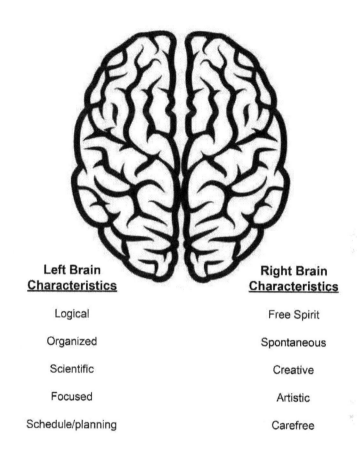

Left Brain Characteristics	**Right Brain Characteristics**
Logical	Free Spirit
Organized	Spontaneous
Scientific	Creative
Focused	Artistic
Schedule/planning	Carefree

We want you to strengthen your strengths, to get highly focused on what you do well, because there are going to be plenty of things in this book for both the left-brained and the right-brained person to attach to that will be easy, that will be joyful, and that they will connect with effortlessly. And do that. Connect. Get focused. Enjoy it. However, as I have seen in my life, and in the thousands of clients that I have worked with over the years, it's when we delve into the uncomfortable, when we hold ourselves accountable to certain daily practices that aren't natural, we see the greatest success. Keep that in mind as we go through the book. When something doesn't feel right, when we are talking about doing a daily practice, and you say, "Oh, that is not for me," just remember, that it's exactly for you. If you follow through with this system, you will absolutely exceed your own expectations in life.

The subconscious mind

In our number one best-selling book on positive thinking, we have devoted an entire chapter about the power of the subconscious mind from both a positive and negative perspective.

If you would like a more detailed description than what I am going to post here, please refer to that book, you will be so happy that you did.

The conscious mind is the mind reading this book. It's the mind that says" I want to change. " It's the mind that sets goals. It's the mind that makes the decision that now is the time to lose weight, get sober, make more money, forgive someone who has hurt us, save your current relationship, change careers or even find a new relationship. That is all the conscious mind.

The subconscious mind is quite different. The subconscious mind only cares about patterns that you have set in life. What you have repeated over and over again in regards to what you eat, drink, how you spend money, how you treat people in life becomes a pattern in the subconscious mind.

The subconscious mind will fight tooth and nail to keep your patterns alive, even if those patterns are not healthy. I can tell you after being an alcoholic and cocaine addict for over 25 years, my conscious mind had the desire to get sober many times, but the subconscious mind continued to battle me, through rationalization, justification and denial to keep me in my addictions until I finally did the action steps necessary to turn the subconscious mind around. To finally be sober and happy for life.

Those things that you do that are healthy, like maybe brushing your teeth every morning and every night, that you would never miss, is the positive side of the subconscious mind. Brushing your teeth has become a pattern, and over the years you would never think about leaving your house or going to bed without brushing your teeth. That is the powerful, positive side of the subconscious mind.

The negative side of the subconscious mind is the saboteur. Remember, all the subconscious mind cares about is the known. The pattern. What you do on a regular basis. And it will fight like hell to keep you in that pattern, regardless if it is healthy or unhealthy.

Now through this book and focus, you can already pretty much imagine that if you start to focus on action steps that may be uncomfortable for us, that will bring you a positive end result, you can slowly start to switch the subconscious mind from saboteur to become your greatest ally.

When we get to the chapter on "The one thing theory" TM, where we describe how to accomplish goals that may have been elusive to you Until now, what we're really doing is attacking the negative side of the subconscious mind. I have rarely seen anyone turn a negative pattern, that is held in the subconscious mind, into a positive and life enhancing pattern via thoughts only.

Now for anyone who woke up one day that had smoked

cigarettes for 30 years and said, "I'm going to stop smoking for the rest of my life today and it's going to be effortless ", and it happened, we call that a miracle. It doesn't happen very often as you can imagine.

The same thing with money. Or losing weight. Or forgiving someone. It normally takes a hell of a lot of work to turn the subconscious mind around, after it has held a negative physical pattern or belief system for a number of years.

That's the power of this system, and that's the power of focus. We have helped thousands of people over the years to radically change their life, by following the program you're reading right now, and changing their subconscious mind set. It will take work. And it will be so worth it.

But let's be forewarned. Any long-term pattern, that you've held in your life, will take consistency, discipline and determination to change. You would never have picked up this book if you weren't ready to change.

And you don't have to be mentally ready to change. This is the message we give our clients every day that I work one on one with as well as on our radio show, and the interviews I do around the world. Even though people say you have to be ready to change before you can change, we say nonsense. I've never met a person, who struggles with any form of addiction, or any other challenge or negative attitude, who started working with me because they were 100% ready to change.

When the subconscious has a negative pattern that it has held onto for years, it loves those kinds of nonsensical theories. It loves when people say that "well I guess I'm just not ready to change, or I would have by now". Remember this, no one is usually ever ready to change a long-term habit that is unhealthy.

So, what do we say to those who say you must be ready to change before you can change? We say it's absolute nonsense, you don't have to be ready to change, you just have to do the work. Daily. Weekly. Monthly.

Surrender to the process in this book. 110%. Don't make excuses. Don't rationalize. Don't justify. Don't deny. Follow everything we're showing you 110%, and I don't care how long you've been challenged in love, with your weight, an Addiction, money or your career... You will change!

Living a Life Lacking Focus

As you read this book, you can probably see that most of us live in a highly unfocused existence, and that is the reason why we don't have what we want in life. Let me give you an example of what this looks like. First of all, if you want to know the classic way to defeat yourself in life, look at the practice of our New Year's resolutions. On New Year's Eve, people make these resolutions for the year; that "I am going to lose weight, quit smoking, save more money, find the love of my life, save my marriage," and they go on, and on, and on, right? It is probably one of the biggest reasons why we never exceed our own expectations in life, because we are not focused. The New Year's Eve resolution system is the most unfocused form of goal setting known to man. And how do we know this? Because twelve months later, for ninety-five percent of people who still set their New Year's resolutions, most of those resolutions are repeated. So, we know it doesn't work.

Another example of how we know that most of us live an unfocused life is the starting and the stopping of projects. And this is classic. How many times have we started to lose weight, and then we stopped? How many times have we gotten excited about going back to church, or temple, or synagogue, and then we stopped? How many times have we made a decision that, this is it; "I am finally going to go back to school, I am finally going to take care of myself, I am finally going to...," fill in the blank. And we started, and we stopped. This unfocused approach to life destroys our own confidence. Going back to confidence and integrity, this is exactly what we are talking about. In the unfocused life, we are not walking our talk. That destroys our internal confidence.

If we really want to see another example of how unfocused many of us are, we just have to look in our closets. Our closets are so cluttered. There was a client that I recently worked with who had twenty-two pairs of jeans, eighteen pairs of flip-flops, thirty jackets, and fifty purses. Now, this might seem extreme, right? But, I would like you right now to put the book down and go into your closet and count how many pairs of shoes and jeans and dresses that you have that you really don't need. See that cluttering? It might be a guy with ten fishing poles. It might be a woman with fifteen extra blankets or thirty towels in the closet, just in case company comes. I remember once working with a woman who on average would have fifteen bottles of shampoo and thirty rolls of toilet paper in her house, when it was just her and her daughter who lived there. Unnecessary. Totally unnecessary.

This cluttering of our physical space continues to knock us off of our focused path. Most of us live a very unconscious existence, and this book is saying, "Let's reel it in." Here is the task to do in your home: go through your closets. Anything that you haven't worn for twelve months, box it up, take it out, clear it up. Do you really need ten pairs of jeans? Do you really need twenty, thirty, or forty pairs of shoes? The answer is no. If you are familiar with the concept of Feng Shui (if you are not familiar with it, Google it; or get the book, "Feng Shui for Dummies"), we know physical clutter also clutters the mind. Go through your house and clear out the clutter, because all of this excess of material goods is destroying your ability to focus. It is robbing you of energy. It is cluttering, not just your physical space, but your brain as well.

Now, let's jump to the office, and it is the same thing. I have worked with clients who have offices at work and at home, and both of them are totally disheveled. I would ask you to do exactly what we do with the clothes: box up all of the files that you don't need for today, and put them in a corner. Twelve months from now, put them in storage, and twelve months from then, if you still don't need them, let them go. Move them out or put them in a storage facility so they are not physically within your eyesight. These simple examples are showing how unfocused many of us are. Remove the excess. It might even be an excess of books in your office, or books at home. Give them away to Goodwill or the Salvation Army. Start to get focused. Get clear to find the energy that you are looking for.

The Power of Writing

The last thing I want to talk about in this chapter is the power of writing, and how we can focus our mind through writing. Remember this, "Don't trust your brain." Wherever in this book that you see a need to stop reading and to write down something that is crucially important for your growth, don't trust your brain and say, "Oh, that is a point I am going to remember." Never trust your brain. Write it down. When we do write our goals down on paper, we begin to get more focused. When we write our goals down, we get very clear on what it is that we are going to do on a daily basis to change our lives.

Also, when we write, messages from the subconscious can come to the surface to give us solutions to challenges. Whatever the blocks or the excuses are, when we write them down, solutions can start to come to the surface, rising from the subconscious, helping us to stay focused and on our path. Writing is an awesome form of accountability.

Yesterday, as a matter of fact, a client came in, and I asked him what he wanted to accomplish. He replied that he wanted to write his first book.

(I love helping people write books. It takes a highly focused approach, and we have a system we teach people on how to do it. Here is the link to learn more: http://davidessel.com/change-your-life-course)

I said, "How long have you been planning on writing this book?" The response was, "About four years now." I said, "Awesome! I would love to see your outline." He tapped the side of his head, and said, "It is right here." I said, "Right where?" He said, "It is in my brain." I then replied, "And that is exactly why you haven't acted on it in four years." It needs to be in writing. Remember, our written plan is a form of accountability. That written plan now says, "It is in the physical world; let's start moving." Otherwise, we can stay in our little fantasy land. When we put all of that in writing, it becomes real. When it is in writing, we have a chance, the very first chance in our lives to actually exceed our own expectations.

Chapter Review

Stop!

Now that you finished this chapter, it is very important that we slow down, and take a few minutes to answer the questions below.

Writing slows the brain down, and allows thoughts from the subconscious to come into consciousness, and this is one way we will take deep advantage of every chapter in this book.

Write. Right now. Let's keep moving towards our goals, with action steps such as these writing exercises, and not rely on our brain to create the life we desire anymore.

1. What was covered in detail, in this chapter?

_____

_____

_____

2. What was of most interest to you and why?

_____

_____

_____

3. What are 1 or 2 actions steps, relevant to the information in this chapter, that you could take right now to help you to focus more in life? Be specific, and also put the exact day and time that you will take these steps.

Focus! Chapter 3:
The One Thing Theory™: The Only Goal-Achievement System You Will Ever Need

"You are worthy of every goal you desire."

In this chapter, I am going to share with you the most powerful goal achievement system you have ever seen. But I'll also say right up front, this program may seem bizarre to a lot of people. And why is that? Because, over the years we have been conditioned. We have been brainwashed. We have been convinced that life balance is possible, and if we go after multiple goals at the same, a little bit every day, life would become perfect. It is hogwash. It is nonsense. It has never worked since the beginning of time, and yet we are still being attracted to programs that promise it will work. It will never work.

What I am going to share with you right now, and I will tell you the story of how we came to create this process, is something that will radically change your life. It will help you to become highly focused and highly successful, and there are millions of people in this world that follow it every day, but many don't realize they are actually doing it. One goal at a time, is the goal. Nothing more. Nothing less. Many of the most common goal setting programs that are available today have great intentions in regards to helping you to accomplish your goals, but they rarely work. Unless we are talking about the highly-discipline, already internally-motivated individuals. And, according to my experience, that is probably about one percent of the world's population. In other words, one percent of the world's population is so highly internally driven that no matter what goal system they follow, it will work. For the rest of us, it hasn't, it won't, and it never will.

Goal Setting Programs that Do Not Work

When I first started doing this work thirty years ago, I was introduced to the "quadrant theory" of goal setting, which is highly common and taught everywhere, even at the finest schools. Some of the most successful individuals in the world promote these two programs that I am going to share with you; the "quadrant program" and the "pie theory" of goal achievement. While they can offer some success along the way, they are highly limited. When I first started teaching as a master life coach, when I first started helping people to transform their lives, I used either the "quadrant theory" or the "pie chart" theory. And for a long period of time, we did see some progress with clients. And let's face it, if you are not focused in life, any type of a program will help you, right? If you are just sort of going through the motions of goal setting, but you don't have a daily plan, and you don't have a daily program, if someone gives you something to follow, you will see some benefits. That is what happened when I became an official life coach in 1991. (In 1996, I altered all of my work to follow what we have created now called The One Thing Theory™.) I used the quadrant and the pie chart to help my clients become more successful. I even used these programs on myself to become more successful. However, here's the caveat: I never was able to reach the highest level of breakthroughs in my professional, personal, career, and finances until I became highly focused, and started following the program we created.

Let me back up and define both the quadrant and pie theory programs in goal setting. The quadrant theory says that we are going to break our life into four major goals: Finances, health, relationships, and spirituality. Then, every week we will choose something to do within each of those areas to help them all improve. In other words, it is kind of like you are juggling four balls in life, and you are trying to keep them all going at the same time. We do a little bit of work on our God path, we do a little bit of work in regards to our financial status, we do a little bit of work with our health, and we do a little bit of work with our relationships. We keep trying to juggle multiple goals at the same time. Now, like I said, I taught this theory for a very long period of time. I saw myself and my clients reach some measurable levels of success. So, again, I will remind you, anything is better than nothing. However, the quadrant system falls short of delivering the success we desire. The other type of system, which is very, very similar, is called the pie theory, or the pie chart system of goal achievement. Here, instead of having four areas of life, we divide life up into six slices of pie. So, we are just getting a little bit more specific.

Instead of saying, just finances, we are going to say finances and career. Instead of just saying our relationships, we are going to say relationships with ourselves and relationships with others. In other words, we add a couple of new categories, but it is the same program. We end up every week saying, "Okay, I am going to do a little bit in each of these six categories of life." I have even seen some goal achievement teachers that will break it up into eight, ten, or twelve slices of the pie, and get very specific, but it is the same bottom line. Instead of four balls of life to try to keep everything going, you are juggling six, eight, ten, or twelve different categories of life. Every day you are looking at your chart and saying, "Okay, did I do a little bit here with my exercise? Did I do a little bit here with God? A little bit with relationship with self? A little bit with relationships with others?" As you can imagine, it eventually will drive you insane. You may see nominal success, if you haven't had any type of organized approach to goal setting, but it is not going to be anything near what it could be if we became highly focused, and just went after one goal at a time.

The One Thing Theory™

I am now going to give you the definition of The One Thing Theory™, and then I will tell you how it came into existence. The One Thing Theory™ is the most highly-focused, goal-achievement program available today. Now, you will notice, I didn't say goal- setting program. It is the most highly-focused, goal-achievement program that the world has ever seen. I am going to say that emphatically because there is nothing, in the thirty years of my doing this work in the world of motivation and personal growth on myself, and then eventually helping millions of other people, I have seen so radically change peoples' lives. I will also give you multiple examples to prove this to be true. The One Thing Theory™ states that at any given time in life, there is only one major goal to go after. It is often the one that we have denied, delayed, or procrastinated taking care of. It is the one that, when we look at it on paper we say, "You know, I don't really have the time to do this. I don't have the money to do this. I don't have the education to do this. I could never forgive that person. I could never...," fill in the blanks for yourself. The One Thing Theory™ states that if we were to attack the one major goal that we don't want to, if we were to finally go after it five days a week for twenty minutes to two hours per day, for a minimal of ninety days, our life would radically change. If the goal is really huge, commit 1 year, 365 days in a row to achieve it, not simply 90 days as we state here. Lose 110+ pounds? Get sober? Double your income? Forgive someone who cheated? Plan on a year of work.

If you believe in the power of focus, like I do, if you look at the Dalai Lamas and the Mother Teresas and the Oprahs of the world; if you look at all of the most successful individuals that have walked this plane, you will see that each of them have followed The One Thing Theory™. You will see that each of them has gone after one major goal in their life that they knew would radically change their whole existence. They attack this "one thing" like a Rottweiler on a bone.

These individuals have become highly successful in life by selecting one area of life to master. If we have one-hundred people in a room, it could be something totally different for each of those one-hundred people. So, my question to you right now is: What have you denied, delayed, or procrastinated working on? What it is that you don't want to face? What is it that will demand of you great effort? What is it, that if you were to attack five days a week for ninety straight days, with an organized, systemized format, would radically change your life? Do you have back taxes that you haven't paid that are weighing on your mind? That could be your one thing. Do you have a resentment against a former lover? Maybe you still have to interact with them because of kids. But, if you were to be able to let go of the resentment, your life would be filled with peace. Do you have resentment against someone who sexually abused you? Or financially abused you? Or maybe emotionally abused you in the past, and that whenever their name comes up, you get the shivers? You also know that if you let go of that resentment, your life would radically change. Do you have a dependency on alcohol, smoking, spending, prescription drugs? Do you have incredible debt or high expenses on a weekly basis that rob you of the inner peace and of being financially free? That could be your one thing. Are you like the seventy percent of Americans who are overweight or obese?

You must know that if you would finally lose that weight once and for all, your life would radically change, and that you would feel great about yourself. Your confidence would increase. Your health would improve. Your sleep would improve.

Do you see where I am going? Do you see where we are

headed? In other words, no matter what we accomplish in life, if we don't go after the thing we have denied, delayed, or procrastinated, starting today, and take care of this issue, all of the other achievements will be short lived. It is incredible how I have seen this happen. In other words, we will go to self-sabotage if we don't take care of the one thing we have denied, delayed, or procrastinated. Let's say, regarding our weight, we might lose ten, twenty, thirty, or forty pounds, but guess what, it is coming back. It is absolutely coming back if we don't take care of the finances, the debt, the over expenditures on a daily basis that rob you of financial security; because the underlying stress will cause emotional eating and the weight you lost will return. You have seen those statistics that say if you get a two-dollar coffee every day, that over the course of four years, it adds up to thousands of dollars of expenses. We might look at our bank account today saying, "Oh my God. If I had those thousands of dollars right now that I have spent in the last five years on this coffee every day, I wouldn't be in the debt I'm in."

Your one thing might be for you, your daily expenses. Or, it could be the release of a resentment against God. That might be your one thing. It could be getting out of victimhood. Maybe you are sitting here, and you are blaming the presidency, or the economy for your bad financial luck, or you are blaming the housing market. Maybe your one thing is to let go of all resentments and get out of the victim mentality. I don't know what it is for you, but I can tell you this: If you are willing to do a little bit of work; if you are willing to get focused to go after and attack this one thing, your life will radically change. On the other hand, if we keep avoiding, denying, or procrastinating taking care of that one issue that has been holding us back, that has been nagging us, that is always sitting in the subconscious; if we do not go after and attack this, we will never reach the highly-focused end result that you and I want, that is in the title of this book. In other words, we will never exceed our own expectations.

For some people, The One Thing Theory™ will lead you to a new belief system about money. This belief system about money might be wrapped up, as Harv Eker says in "Secrets of the Millionaire Mind," in the fact that money is the root of all evil, that rich people are greedy, and that it is better to give than receive. All of those ridiculous statements, that have no basis in reality, are holding you back financially. It is amazing how The One Thing Theory™ works. Let's go to the Bible for a minute. When we talk about multiple goals; when we talk about the quadrant theory or the pie chart theory of goal setting, just think about what Jesus said in the Bible, when he refers to the fact that you cannot serve two masters at once. So, you cannot serve money and love. What is the correct quote out of the Bible? It is not that money is the root of all evil. The correct quote out of the Bible is, "The love of money is the root of all evil." In other words, if you put money up on a pedestal, and you love it so much, you are willing to do whatever it takes that may even be against your morals and ethics; cheating on your taxes, for an example, not reporting all of your income, or fabricating expenses. Okay, well you have just created another master. So, love is not your master; spirituality is not your master, and God is not your master, because love, spirituality, and God are all based in honesty. Do you follow me here? So, all of a sudden you are serving two masters. Your greed, your love of money, has overcome your moral and ethical decision making, which is going to come back, and it's going to bite you in the butt. Later on, we will talk about karma, to see how we can clean our lives up at an even deeper level.

For now, you can also watch a video I created to learn more about The One Thing Theory™ here:
http://davidessel.com/life-relationship-business-coach

Let's go back to the statement: "You cannot serve two

masters at the same time." That falls perfectly into The One Thing Theory™. In our belief system, you cannot serve two goals at the same time. No one has the energy to put one hundred percent effort into two goals. So, in other words, if someone comes to me and says, "You know what, David? I really need to lose twenty-five pounds, and I want to forgive my parents for some type of abuse," or "I want to earn one hundred thousand dollars a year, and at the same time, I want to create this amazing pathway to God," or, "I want to find the love of my life, and at the same time, I want to find a new career path," I will work with those people and they will quickly see that we can only serve one goal at a time. The One Thing Theory™ is unbelievably powerful. They will see for themselves that we can't serve two masters, that they are going to have to make a decision on which of the goals in front of them will have the most powerful effect on their life. Which of the two goals have they denied, delayed, or procrastinated the longest? Sometimes people come in with three, or four, or five goals. Which of those three, or four, or five goals have we denied, delayed, or procrastinated working on the longest that will radically change our existence? That is the master we want to serve. That is the one goal, the one master that we want to go after.

The Interview That Changed My Life

I had an interview in 1996 that led to me create this whole process around focus and The One Thing Theory™ that radically changed every area of my life forever. I will never forget the interview. At that time, I hosted a nationally syndicated radio talk show with Westwood One. We were in about 230 cities across the United States. It had just exploded. Our audience base was huge. We were interviewing the greatest minds, the most incredibly successful people in this world in the realm of finances, spirituality, fitness, career, relationships, love, you name it. We had the most positively outrageous interviews back then, just like we do now. During that year, we had an opportunity to interview an individual named Maharishi Mahesh Yogi. Maharishi Mahesh Yogi was the founder of transcendental meditation.

If you remember in the late fifties and early sixties, the Beatles became huge proponents of transcendental meditation, and spread the message around the world, as they still do today. As a matter of fact, several years ago, Paul McCartney offered a free concert in Central Park, and the purpose of the concert was to continue to promote the benefits of transcendental meditation. Our own government, as well as so many other organizations, have done studies, double-blind placebo-controlled studies on the power of Transcendental Meditation and its positive effects on our mind, addiction recovery, reversing the aging process, attitude, and so much more. This stuff works.

Maharishi, who has since passed, was based then in Holland, with his University in Fairfield, Iowa. I had been doing Transcendental Meditation for a number of years, and I was blown away at the changes that had happened in my life due to this daily practice.

When I had the chance to interview the founder of TM, I

was ecstatic. It was the fortieth anniversary of transcendental meditation, and Maharishi and his organization searched across America for one media outlet to do an interview with to celebrate this milestone, and they chose our show, David Essel ALIVE! in order to do that. My team at David Essel ALIVE! was amazed that, of all of the other avenues that Maharishi had, television shows and radio shows other than ours, that they selected us. We were highly honored.

As we went through the interview, Maharishi was amazing, just unbelievably amazing. The interview was so much fun. It was filled with laughter and joy, and also some highly esoteric principles. When he would start to discuss them, quite frankly at that time, many were going over my head. We would then go to another question, and we would be laughing, and I would be spellbound. He would explain these incredibly difficult concepts of why we are here, including evolution, awakening, and enlightenment. I would just sit there and say, "Oh my Lord. This guy is incredible."

Three weeks later, I am in Orlando, Florida, speaking at a convention, and as I come off stage, a woman came up to me and asked me if she could buy me coffee and talk about my presentation. As we are having coffee, she said, "Listen, I want to ask you about an interview you did a couple of weeks ago with Maharishi Mahesh Yogi," which I was more than excited to discuss. When I asked her why, she said, "Well, I have been with Maharishi for thirty-six of his forty years, since he created Transcendental Meditation and started promoting it around world." Then she went on to ask me what I remembered from the interview. I could not remember anything, other than the fact that this man was filled with so much joy and love. It was very weird because, when I would interview Deepak Chopra, or Wayne Dyer, or Suze Orman, or athletes, or movie stars, like Jenna Elfman, or incredible authors, like Mark Victor

Hansen, from "Chicken Soup for the Soul," I would always remember the four major points they covered, or the six major points they covered, or the one major point they covered. I always had a great memory of stories that people would share with me, and I could easily say to this woman sitting in front of me, "Oh, you know, when I interviewed so and so, this was their main point," but when it came to her question regarding Maharishi, I had no answer.

Finally, I looked at her, and I said, "You know, I don't really remember anything other than joy and laughter from Maharishi, and it is kind of strange that that's all I can remember." She smiled and said, "David, that's because you don't have any joy in your life." I looked at her, and I was aghast at her reply. My small ego started going on and on in my head, "Who does this woman think she is? She doesn't even know me. I have been talking to her for fifteen minutes. She doesn't have a clue of who I am, and she is telling me I have no joy. You've got to be kidding me." I continued speaking to her, but in the back of my mind I am saying, "I'm going to get out of this conversation very quickly, because this woman obviously doesn't know me." As we talked more, I finally said that. "You know, I think you have come to a conclusion, and that you really don't know what you are talking about, because you don't know me, and yet you are making this claim that I don't have joy." My feathers were ruffled. My small ego was hurt. She went on then to explain her point. "David, listen, please don't take it personally. It is just the truth. Whenever myself and other followers of Maharishi would be with him, we might be sitting in a room and he would speak for four, five, six, seven, or eight hours. We would walk out of the room and collectively start asking each other what we got out of the presentation, and almost every time it was the same thing. People would talk about different topics that he covered, and the rest of us would say, I don't remember him even covering that topic."

"The point, David, is this: Whatever it is that you walk out remembering that Maharishi said, is what is lacking from your life."

You can imagine that I was not a big fan of hers. I was sitting there thinking, "How can she say now that I have no joy in my life, just because these things happened to her and her colleagues when they were sitting with Maharishi." Well, needless to say, I wrapped up the conversation pretty quickly. I was very polite and very nice, but I really wasn't buying it. Weeks go by, and the thought kept coming through my mind that she had just shared: "David, the only thing you will take out of an interview or a conversation with Maharishi, is that which is lacking from your life." So, I continued to run that through my brain, and I sat there trying to intellectually understand it. I said to myself, "But wait a minute; I host the most positive and the most popular positive radio show across the United States of America every week. I have just written my first book. My client base from my 1-on-1 coaching clients is off the wall; I have a waiting list. I live on the beach. I have a Mercedes convertible." I went down this list of all of this stuff, and I said, "You know, I just don't see it. Maybe what she is saying is true for other people, but it is not for me." It was about six weeks later that I woke up one day and I got it; she was right. I had very little joy in my life. I was addicted to multiple things: Number one - work, number two—fame, number three—money, number four—alcohol, and number five, I was a binge cocaine addict.

Now, all of those things wrapped together would make it obvious to anyone in the outside world that maybe she was right, that just maybe I didn't have the joy I thought I had. As the days continued to go by, the epiphany of understanding that she was right was impossible to ignore and I knew I had to start working on something to radically change my own life. So, I started looking at it. What is my one thing? What is the thing that I have denied, delayed, or procrastinated working on for the longest? What is the thing that is absolutely destroying me? What is the thing that I need to let go of right away in order to feel joy? As I looked at this list of all of these things that I eventually had to attack, I knew I could only do one at a time. This was the birthplace of The One Thing Theory™. The very first thing I had to attack was my binge cocaine addiction. Now, I had this addiction since college, and even though I was working with addicts and helping people to get clean, every several months I would hide away with a several-day blast, a binge of my addictive process with cocaine. I would be gone from society for several days. In that process, I would be up all night. I would be trying to reach that level of "connection" that people experience with a cocaine addiction, or any addiction for that matter, that we believe can only be reached with an outside substance. I needed an awakening. And it came on a Tuesday, in 1996, after the interview with Maharishi, after the connection with this woman who was one of his colleagues. A Tuesday afternoon at 2:30 p.m.; I remember it like it was yesterday. I had only been to sleep for about four hours, and I awoke in so much pain from my latest binge from the several days before, and I knew that I could not carry on like this anymore. My joy was absolutely ripped out of my life. She was right, and Maharishi was right. On that very day, I screamed out to God for the one thousandth time to take this addiction away. I have no idea how it happened, other than my intense prayer, on my knees, screaming for salvation, screaming for recovery.

Something clicked at that time, an awakening and awareness. I do praise God from that day forward, because my first "one thing" was healed.

When I realized that the awareness of the addiction was a pathway to freedom, joy and success, I literally changed my life on that day. I also started working on changing my philosophy with coaching my 1-on-1 clients, throwing out the pie charts and the quadrant theory, and working on The One Thing Theory™. It was also in that year, 1996, that my life coach certification program was created, where I started to certify people to become life coaches. Out of that, "Life Coach Universe™" would be born, an official organization that trains people to become coaches. In that process, just like in this book, the anchor, the one thing that we train our coaches on to go and help others with, that separates our life coach training certification from all other certifications in the world, is the process of The One Thing Theory™.

When this breakthrough occurred in 1996, I knew that I had to share this with the world, which we have been doing since then. Everything changed in that year; everything about the way I worked 1-on-1 with my clients and the way that I lived with my own life. As I go through my existence, I continue to knock off my one-things, the things I have denied, delayed, or procrastinated working on in my own life, like my various addictions. There was one time I had to really focus on finances. There was another time that I had to really focus on my health. There was another time that I had to focus on my codependency with others, my craving to be accepted by everyone I met. Every time I do this, I see my life go to a whole new level, just like it has been happening since 1996 with all of my clients. This system is so powerful. This system will blow away your beliefs in regards to what you are capable of achieving. I know, since it has worked for thousands upon thousands of people since we started it, that it will work for you as well.

What is Your One Thing?

So, what is your one thing? We have created a list of six areas of life for you to choose your one thing from:

- The first area of life is relationship with self.

- The second area of life is your career.

- The third area of life is your health.

- The fourth area of life is your spiritual path or religious path.

- The fifth area of life is your finances.

- The sixth area of life is your relationship with others.

Look at the list, consider each of these areas and say, "Which of these have I denied, delayed, or procrastinated working on? Which of these areas have I not wanted to face? Which of these areas, that if I were to move through and accomplish, would I breathe easier, sleep better, feel better, would I create more success in my life?" That is the area we want you to focus on. Remember, you cannot exceed your expectations in life if we are not willing to remove those anchors that are holding us back. This is the key to our work. In other words, some people will say, "I know that if I was free financially, if I just earn 250 thousand dollars a year, my life would be so radically changed." We know that is not true. The example that proves this is erroneous thinking that is so often used is with lottery winners. According to a Gallup poll, about forty percent of individuals who win the lottery are bankrupt within four to five years. So, this tells us that money isn't the answer. There is something deeper that has to be taken care of; and that usually is beliefs about money, being worthy of receiving from this world. Remember that old adage, "it is better to give than to receive;" well, it is not true. It is better to give and to receive.

Unless we have this clear belief system around money, no matter how much money you make, you will always lose it. It will be rollercoaster, the yo-yo; make money and lose money, out of debt and in debt. It goes back and forth constantly. So, what we want to do with The One Thing Theory™ is say, "What is this thing about money?" and go deeper into it. Hire someone, or use our programs, to help you see what you cannot see by yourself regarding resentments, regarding belief systems about your body, money, addiction, or whatever it might be. This is the key to our program. I just want to say this again: If it wasn't so effective, we couldn't be doing this since 1996. It really, really works.

Now, take a moment in the spaces below and write down the area of life, from the six areas we listed above, where your "one thing" resides:

_____

_____

_____

Be specific with this exercise. If you're one thing is in the health category, write down the health concern i.e. sobriety or weight loss or high blood pressure. Don't leave it in a very broad category. The more specific, the easier it will be to set up your action steps to radically change your life.

Client Stories

Here are some examples of just a few of our clients who have mastered their life, who have exceeded their own expectations by focusing on The One Thing Theory™.

Tracy lost eighty pounds and has kept it off for 8 years already. When we worked together, her one thing was health, without a doubt. She had three young kids. She was working, and her husband worked, and their relationship was strained at the time. Of course, she was one of those people who were always doing for others, but her one thing wasn't finding more time in the day. It wasn't making more money. It was her health. So, she went on this incredible program, highly focused, to lose this weight. Within eight weeks, she had lost twenty-four pounds. Within a year, she had lost eighty pounds, and she has kept it off. Her life has radically changed. That is like losing almost a full person that you are carrying around, right? Can you imagine someone who needed to lose eighty pounds, how much better they would feel about themselves by losing that weight? The other thing that Tracy did while she was losing the weight, in our work together, is that she got to the core beliefs about worthiness of losing the weight and how to create that pathway to success that she could sustain. Many people who don't figure out the concept of self-sabotage and goal setting will lose the weight and gain it back. Tracy has still kept the eighty pounds off, and her life has radically changed.

I worked with a couple once who were trying to recover from an affair. When they came in, of course, the one thing that they originally thought was going to be the core of their work was who was "really" to blame. "He did this to me," "she did that to me." But, their real one thing is going to be shocking to many people. When they focused on, "What was my role in this affair?" "How did my lack of communication lead to this affair? "What was it that I did that pushed my husband out of my house to have an affair with someone else?" and, "What was I not communicating to my wife, that I held resentments about, that led me to have the affair?" Their one thing, is called self-responsibility. When they both found their one thing, and they both became responsible for their actions that led to the affair, their marriage healed. Now, this is a couple I worked with 10 years ago, and their marriage and their love are more solid and deeper than they had ever had in the eighteen years of marriage prior to finding their one thing.

So, the one thing with this couple, which is very difficult to admit and honestly deal with when there has been an affair, was simple, powerful, and difficult: "What was my role in this affair, and how do I admit it and release it?" That is what each of those people had to do in order to create the deepest love they have ever experienced. Now, for most people, after an affair, whoever cheated, whoever went out and had the physical contact with someone else, is who we blame. The victim is the person who is pointing the finger. The person who actually had sex with someone else is the one who we want to hang. It is just the bottom line, it is the way life works, even though it doesn't "really" work that way. In actuality, what this couple did was very brave, strong and powerful.

I have worked with many, many couples over the past twenty-plus years that have had to come to this conclusion, that if I don't take my responsibility, look at, and release it, for how this relationship crumbled, I am going to repeat the pattern, hold the resentment, and repeat it in the future. They attacked their one thing and, obviously, the result is amazing.

Another great example of someone who went after the one thing was Angela. In ninety days, Angela doubled her income, even though she did not have a college education. In her case, her one thing was money, because she was making so little that it was a stressor in every area of her life. Her one thing was increasing her income. So, we went through all of her belief systems around money, worked through them, and then we created a plan of attack. Her one thing was to double her income. Now, she has said to me, and I have repeated this thousands of times to audiences I have spoken to, that she was not convinced it was possible. Just like a lot of people I work with who don't think that sobriety is going to be possible because they have been drinking for so long, or don't think that forgiveness is going to be possible because they've held resentments for so long, or who, like Angela, don't think they are going to actually be able to double their income. So, we worked on Angela's beliefs, and then we got into the plan. In ninety days, she doubled it, but it even gets better. It was ninety days, to the day, when she got the offer that doubled her income, and wouldn't you know it, three days later she called me back and said, "David, I am so stressed. You are not going to believe what happened. I got another offer at more than double my income." Then a couple days later, well you guessed it, she got another offer that was even higher than that. Her income continues to skyrocket. She is doing amazing things in life, and it is all because she focused on her one thing.

The last little story I am going to share with you is about someone who achieved great success with The One Thing Theory™ is a client named Howard. Howard came to me with thirty-plus years of heavy alcohol addiction. He was a highly-functioning alcoholic. He was able to own his home and keep a job, but a serious alcoholic nonetheless. Within eight weeks of intense work together, Howard was able to get into recovery and to experience sobriety. That was a number of years ago, and he is still sober today.

I want to say this again: When most people come in to work with our program, they are not aware of The One Thing Theory™. They are not aware of choosing one goal and going after only one goal at a time. They are only aware that life is not working. When we explain the system that you are reading about right now, when we explain the power of focus, and when we explain that if they were to get the focus, find the one thing, and do the work, they would exceed even their own expectations in life. Well, sometimes people honestly are skeptical. We have thousands of stories proving this system absolutely works.

Critical Steps: Focus For Success

1. Pick one goal

2. Write an action plan for this goal 5-7 days per week

3. Walk through fire to make this happen. No excuses ever!

4. Hire an accountability partner. Be honest and do what they tell you.

If you really want to change, I will offer you a free 15-minute one-on-one phone session at no charge!

Email us today and one of my assistants will set this up for you. Just go to our website **www.davidessel.com** and send us an email via the contact us button.

We will get you moving in the direction of your dreams, and help you get focused on the most important goal in your life.

Important!

If your goal is smaller, say to lose 25 pounds, commit to a 90-day program in order to do this. A full 90-day commitment, no excuses, will get you there!

However, if your goal is huge, say to lose 100 pounds, commit, no excuses, to 365 days in a row. Success will be yours if you focus on only one goal at a time.

Chapter Review

Stop!

Now that you finished this chapter, it is very important that we slow down, and take a few minutes to answer the questions below.

Writing slows the brain down, and allows thoughts from the subconscious to come into consciousness, and this is one way we will take deep advantage of every chapter in this book.

Write. Right now. Let's keep moving towards our goals, with action steps such as these writing exercises, and not rely on our brain to create the life we desire anymore.

1. What was covered in detail, in this chapter?

_____

_____

_____

2. What was of most interest to you and why?

_____

_____

_____

3. What are 1 or 2 actions steps, relevant to the information in this chapter, that you could take right now to help you to focus more in life? Be specific, and also put the exact day and time that you will take these steps.

_____

_____

_____

Focus! Chapter 4:
Focus and Accountability: How to Exceed Your Own Expectations in Life

"You are worthy of every goal you desire."

We rarely accomplish any major goals in life by ourselves. Did you ever realize that? One of the reasons that this is true is because of the concept of accountability. With our program on focus, accountability is everything. It is actually quite the opposite of what the human brain wants to do. In other words, what we would really like to be able to do is lose the weight, make the money, get sober, find the love of our lives, enhance our current relationships, save our marriage, or get closer to God, all by ourselves. Most of us don't want to be held accountable. We do not want someone to be saying, "Did you do this today?" "Did you follow through with those calls today?" Did you get into the gym today?" Did you watch what you ate all day long?" "Did you deal with the anxiety, instead of going and having a drink?" Whatever we want to accomplish in life, first, we need to first get focused, and then, we need to be held accountable to change.

One of the reasons that there are life coaches and athletic coaches, counselors, therapists, and ministers, is because of the importance of accountability. Over the years, in our world of counseling and life coaching, we have really fine-tuned this concept of accountability to make it much different than any other forms of 1-on-1 personal growth or self-help programs. If you look back years ago, when we would work with counselors, or therapists, or ministers, the normal scenario would be, "This was a great session. I look forward to seeing you in seven days. Keep in mind everything that we talked about." That was it. Now it has radically changed. In our life coach certification courses, we emphasize the need to hold our clients accountable. We train our teachers how to do that through writing exercises, and through questions that go deep into the aspect of why we want to change and how we are going to change. And, the next step is crucial. The coaches that we train, as well as the clients that I work with, have certain deadlines to hit in their accountability process in order to accomplish what they want in life. There is no more of the "old-day approach" to coaching, where we would say to someone, "That was a great session. I can't wait to see you next week." That doesn't work. It really never worked. Now what we say is, "That was a great session. Here are the assignments to do over the next seven days. I want you to answer these questions in writing. I want these homework assignments to be sent to me within twenty-four hours, or forty-eight hours, or seventy-two hours. Keep a diary or a log of all of the tasks that you have done to accomplish your goal for the next seven days. Bring all of this in next week, and we will go over it." That is called accountability; and this is an important part of all powerful goal achievement programs.

When we add this component of accountability, and you follow what we are encouraging you to do in this book, you can absolutely exceed your own expectations in life. But we need to find someone to hold us accountable. We need an accountability coach or an accountability partner. We need an accountability professional who is going to be there with us step-by-step. If we do not follow through on tasks that we say we are going to do, we have to have someone calling us out on the table, and saying, "If you are serious and you want to keep working together, you have to do the work, period; or you may want to find someone else to work with." Now, that is what I call a true accountability coach.

Remember, we rarely accomplish any great things in our life by ourselves. I don't know too many people over the history of time that are incredibly focused and successful who do it by themselves. Stephen King has worked with editors and publishers to become one of the most prolific authors of all time. Michael Jordan, I remember in an interview one time, when someone said, "What does it feel like to be called the greatest basketball player of all time, to be able to do this by yourself with your God-given talents?" He looked at the interviewer and said, "I wish I could say that is the case, but it is not. I have surrounded myself with the best coaches, the best nutritionists, the best personal trainers, and the best mental toughness coaches that I can find to be able to do what I have done on the basketball court." Do you see what I mean? We don't do these things alone.

Whatever it is that you want to accomplish in life, your "one thing," you will definitely need an accountability partner to make it happen. You might be thinking right now: "If I could just forgive this person", or "forgive myself." "If I could just make X amount of dollars." "If I could just lose this weight." "If I could just open my own business that I have dreamt about for years", or "write that book." "If I could just save my marriage", or "rebuild my relationship with my children." "If I could just get sober", or "find that incredible loving relationship I've always wanted." Or maybe, "If I could just find inner peace by developing a deep, abiding relationship with God." Whatever your goal is, you're going to have to find someone to help you accomplish it. Again, let me repeat this: We rarely accomplish any substantial goals in life alone, which means, you probably will not exceed your own expectations if you try to do it by yourself.

You see with accountability, we can't hide. Everything is out there. We can't say that we are eating perfectly, and we are exercising as we need to, when we have an accountability coach who is weighing us or measuring our body every four weeks. Maybe there is no movement on the scale, or there is no movement on the tape. They will look at us and say, "Okay, wait a second. There is something you're not doing, or this scale would've moved by now", or "these measurements would've changed." Do you know what I'm saying? We need an accountability partner to make these dreams our reality.

Who Will Be Your Accountability Partner?

I'm going to get you involved right now in finding your accountability partner. I want you to write this down: Who do you need to reach out to in order to accomplish your biggest goal in life? Look at the list below, choose who you need to work with. Who will be your accountability partner in order to accomplish your greatest goal in life?

Will it be:
1. A life coach?
2. A minister?
3. A counselor or a therapist?
4. A financial adviser?
5. A mentor?
6. A personal trainer?
7. A massage therapist, or some type of energy healer?

Now, when you look at that list, I want you to just put a check mark in the book next to maybe one or two of those types of individuals that you know you need to contact to ask them to be a part of your accountability process. Who do you want to be your accountability partner in order to achieve your greatest goal?

Do not, I repeat, do not trust your brain when it says, "You know what, David, that's great for most people, but I know I can do this on my own." If you could've done it on your own, you already would have. The fact that we still have huge goals to accomplish says we are not going to be able to do it on our own, and we need to reach out for help.

The next step, after you choose who you are going to work with, is to go ahead and figure out a date and time we are going to begin the process. Write that down now. What day and what time will you hire this person, or will you trade services and barter with this person, to become your professional accountability partner? Don't just read this book and nod your head and say, "Oh this is great," and "That will work." It is more important than ever for us to slow down today and to make the decisions in order to, yes, exceed our own expectations.

On a side note, I want to make a comment about friends and family members as accountability partners. We rarely recommend doing this. Most of the time, when we have friends or family members who become our accountability partners, it leads to nothing but chaos and drama. Even though they have their best intentions at heart, too many times family members or friends will fall into one of two categories. They will become the drill sergeant. Because of their desire to help you succeed, and also because of their lack of training in knowing how to push people to certain limits and hold them there, they could go over the top and actually damage the friendship or relationship. The second way that individuals who are friends or family members might sabotage your success, unknowingly, is that they do not hold you accountable enough. They are not strongly based in accountability principles, so they let you get away with more things than a professional would. I would highly recommend that you look at the list once again and find professionals, and actually hire them to help you achieve your greatest goals.

In the realm of mentorship, there are mentors around the world that you may be able to work with at no charge. There are many people that I know that have mentored me because they've wanted to see my level of success rise dramatically. They believed in me. And, over the course of years, I've done the same. That is an avenue you may want to pursue, as well as pursing a professional to hire. In this very moment, as I write this book, I can tell you I have multiple accountability partners in my life; some that I pay, and some that I will do an exchange of services, offering them the same support in their growth that they offer to me. Regardless of how it is done, there is no way in my life that

I am going to exceed my expectations, even though I work in this field, without powerful accountability partners.

Clients Who Committed to Accountability

I want to share a few more stories of individuals whom I have worked with who became very focused and successful in life. They asked to be held accountable for their own personal growth, through the various programs we offer, and have once again exceeded their own expectations. While I love to talk about the Harv Ekers, and the Michael Jordans, the Walt Disneys, and the Suze Ormans of the world, I also want to share within this book people that are achieving exceptional levels of success that you may never hear of, but nonetheless, they are inspirational to me today, and I hope to you as well.

In the world of spirituality, I met a client named Lynne, who came in looking for assistance with her marriage. When she first walked in the door, and she would admit this to this day, her real purpose was to see if I would agree with her that, in her mind, her husband had dropped the ball in their relationship, and it might be time for her to leave.

We worked for multiple weeks on this very topic, and by doing intense exercises that I had given her after every session, she came to the realization that maybe it wasn't her husband's fault entirely for the breakdown of their relationship, for the disintegration of their marriage. She also found out that, if she were to apply principles that we were talking about in the sessions in her marriage, that she might be able to resurrect it. Lynne exceeded her own expectations by doing the most incredibly challenging work that anyone in relationships will do, and that is to look at her role in the dysfunction. She not only looked at her role, but she took an accountability approach to it, changed her role, and ultimately, not only saved, but created a love and a marriage she never knew possible.

When we worked through that, we came up to her next "one thing." Lynne's desire was to become one with the divine, to become one with God, and to experience God on a daily basis. An awesome goal; one that you can imagine offers incredible benefits in any and every area of an individual's life. As we went through and decided upon what Lynne's daily rituals would be and the practices to open her heart and to become closer to God, we came to this "block" regarding time. Finding the time to do this was a real challenge for her. She not only was working very deeply on her marriage, and successfully so, but she had several children and a business she was running. She could not find the time in her day in order to create this space to deepen her spiritual path.

Through our work together and holding her accountable, one of the exercises I gave her was to go and block out her days, and to come back with one hour per day that she knew she would be able to devote to her practice of spirituality. Seven days later, she comes walking in, smiling and shaking her head, and saying, "The only time, David, that is even possible is 5 a.m., and I don't even know if I can do that." As her accountability coach, there was only one thing for me to say to her, "Let's go." Her eyes got really big as she realized it was the only step she needed to take in order to bring this goal to her own realization and to exceed her expectations. Well, we are talking five or six years later now, and Lynne continues to get up earlier than the birds every morning, and her spiritual path has become her foundation for her own personal success in life. And yes, her relationship with God has deepened so greatly that she has now used this as an opportunity as a professional master life coach to powerfully affect the lives of thousands of people in this world today.

Lynne would be the first one to share with you right now that without an accountability partner, whether it was me or someone else, the odds of accomplishing this goal would not have been possible.

Next, will be Lisa, who came to me as a heavy long-term addict of alcohol and drugs, from pain pills to heroin to crack cocaine. She was also a heavy smoker and drinker. I can't imagine a substance that she had not been battling. Lisa came to me a few months after ending a rehab program and was in desperate need of daily accountability, even if at that moment she didn't know how radically her life would change. The accountability factor, when I work with someone five days a week, is intensely high. They know that the next day when they call me on the phone, or they come into my office, that they have work that needed to be done since the end of our session twenty-four hours earlier. Lisa had never experienced this form of accountability before. When you look at someone with thirteen years of heavy drug and alcohol addiction, who is only thirty years old at the time, with two young children, the odds of succeeding are incredibly small, unless they are willing to hold themselves accountable and surrender one hundred percent to someone else's program.

For twenty years prior to meeting and working with Lisa, we found that our program, which is holistically based (meaning that we work from a mind, body, spirit, nutrition, exercise perspective, as well as deep emotional healing), we knew that if anyone were to apply the principles that we offered them they could become successful, regardless of how intense or how long their addiction had been going on for. Within days, Lisa, a long-time smoker, had dropped her nicotine habit. She had lost her cravings for the needles and the drugs. It wouldn't be that the cravings didn't come back down the road, but in her eyes, she was amazed that within a period of seven days, then fourteen days, then twenty-one, that for the first time in her life that she can imagine, she began to feel free. I look at people like Lisa as absolute miracles in life.

The exercises that I gave her on a daily basis were always

completed one hundred percent. She has become one of the shining stars of our holistic addiction recovery program. Of the many, many people we've worked with, and the many successes we have, Lisa is by far right up at the top of the list, because she had such a long history of intense drug and alcohol use, and such a long history of emotional issues that had not been dealt with. From that time forward, when she completed our program, she has gone on to win back the custody of her children that she had lost during her drug abuse years, as well as pass medical boards and become a healthcare professional. It is unbelievable the success she has achieved through the power of an accountability program.

John, is another success story when it came to accountability. He was a very, very successful professional, but over the years he had never really paid attention to the concept of financial freedom, budgeting, income, expenses and more.

After seeing his pattern of being stressed around money return year after year after year, he decided to join our financial freedom program and the results, because of his incredible hard work, and willingness to be held accountable every week were amazing.

Imagine this, and maybe this is you, he had never written down in any type of detail on a daily basis how much he was spending. He never really recorded his weekly or monthly income, in order to compare it to his expenses. But I could tell how serious he was, within seven days.

At the end of the first week he came in with every penny spent. And I mean every penny. I had introduced him to the concept of financial wants and needs... Which is something most of us don't want to pay attention to.

So after every expense in his notebook, he had to write if it was a "want" or a "need". A "want" is something that is not necessary for us to survive. So instead of bringing your lunch to work, you go out for lunch every day and end up spending $10, $15 or $20 a day and when added up that can totally sabotage much of your financial freedom.

When we were going over his weekly expenses, he was laughing the whole time saying, "I know this is only the first week, but because I had to actually write everything I spent down, and was it a want or need, it woke me up to realize that I waste so much of my money every year."

Every week for the next 10 weeks John came in fully prepared. He ended up doing charts, diagrams and blowing my mind about how serious he took it. Every page in the manual was totally filled out. The books I recommended were read. He knew, that when he came in on a weekly basis I would be expecting him to complete the homework and he did it in a brilliant way.

And, it even gets better. His wife was absolutely thrilled. And she let him know, as well as myself, how proud she was that he was willing to surrender his old belief systems about money and accountability to a brand-new program, and the results were literally instantaneous. But they were only instantaneous because he surrendered to the program of accountability, the missing link in our desire for success in life.

Marianne was frustrated with her own lack of emotional self-control. When I first started working with her, she was convinced that most of her frustrations in life were because of other people, not herself. But, as I was soon to find out, here was another client that was ready to commit to this work like a honey badger.

One of the hardest things for all of us to do is to take accountability for the dysfunction in our life, and look for all the signs that say that we are playing a bigger role in our own frustration that we may think. And Marianne was like millions of people, who was projecting blame on everyone else and until we started working together could not accept responsibility for her frustrations in life.

One of the exercises that I gave her was to go back as far as she could remember, to try to recall when her temper became an issue in life. I could tell once again that she was serious, because of the detail she put into every week's homework assignments.

At the end of three weeks, as she was reading the assignments to me over the phone, a lightbulb went off in her head. She was amazed at the pattern she was reading in her own writing. She was amazed that she was the centerpiece of so much of her anger and rage, and because of her willingness to follow through with every assignment given to her... Her attitude began to change quite quickly.

She saw how she would overreact to the simplest of frustrations. If it was her husband, or one of her four children, her mother, father, mother-in-law or father-in-law, before being held accountable to do this kind of detailed homework, none of the blowups were her fault... Or so she thought... But after being held accountable for a number of weeks she could literally look in the mirror and point her finger at the person causing so much of the dysfunction.

Now this doesn't mean that all these other people in her life played no role in her blowups, but she saw, that her overreaction to their words, was creating hell on earth for her.

And how did she get to this realization so quickly? Many people can work with a counselor or a coach for years before the walls come down, before they can become this vulnerable, and look at the reality of what they're bringing into this world regarding what might not be working for them. It was her willingness to go deep into the writing assignments every week, and never coming up with an excuse as to why she didn't have time to do the assignments given to her. Again, a little honey badger in the world of personal growth.

At the end of six months, the people around her were amazed at the changes she was making in her life. As she continued to call in for her sessions, almost every other week she was telling me that someone in her family was complementing her on how her emotional responses to life changed so dramatically. Two of her sons, who had created emotional walls against their own mom, started to open up and tell her that they wanted to spend more time with her. As she was reading to me the responses of her family members, I have to admit, tears were streaming down my face.

Accountability, is the last missing key for many people who want to become successful in life. It's not easy. The subconscious mind will push back, and tell us that we don't need to hire someone to work through our own issues. But when you do, the world begins to shape up in a whole new way, and many times, very quickly.

Here is a video on choosing an accountability partner that may help: http://davidessel.com/life-relationship-business-coach

If you, as you read this book, truly want to change your life and exceed your own expectations, it will have to be done through the help of an accountability professional, a coach, or a partner who will be willing to ask you to do the uncomfortable, to hold your feet to the fire, to do what you may not want to do on your own to create the life you truly want.

Chapter Review

Stop!

Now that you finished this chapter, it is very important that we slow down, and take a few minutes to answer the questions below.

Writing slows the brain down, and allows thoughts from the subconscious to come into consciousness, and this is one way we will take deep advantage of every chapter in this book.

Write. Right now. Let's keep moving towards our goals, with action steps such as these writing exercises, and not rely on our brain to create the life we desire anymore.

1. What was covered in detail, in this chapter?

_____

_____

_____

2. What was of most interest to you and why?

_____

_____

_____

3. What are 1 or 2 actions steps, relevant to the information in this chapter, that you could take right now to help you to focus more in life? Be specific, and also put the exact day and time that you will take these steps.

_____

_____

_____

Focus! Chapter 5:
How to Manifest Your Goals in a Focused Way

"You are worthy of every goal you desire."

Now, where do we go from here? You might be thinking, right now, "What do I do to stay focused? What type of a system can I follow? Once I find that one area of life that I have denied, delayed, or procrastinated, once I've found my accountability partner, what do I do next?" Going back once again to 1996, when I started to do all of my counseling and life coaching in a radically different way in order to help my clients exceed their own expectations, we created something called the 3 Keys to Manifestation. In other words, the three keys to creating the life that you want. I am going to go through these each right now.

The Very First Key, Number One, is Intention.

Intention is a statement of affirmation. It is a statement that says, "This is what I desire to accomplish." Now, we do affirmations/intentions, I use those words interchangeably, very differently. We don't believe in pie-in-the-sky affirmations or intentions. We don't believe in saying, "I earn one hundred thousand dollars a year," if we are currently earning twenty thousand dollars a year. The subconscious does not buy into it. It says, "You've got to be kidding me.

Who are you to repeat every morning that you are earning one hundred thousand dollars a year, when you are earning twenty thousand dollars a year, and you are not doing anything different to create this added income?" That is the way the subconscious takes these ridiculous affirmations that we have all bought into over the years, written by some amazing authors and well-meaning teachers, that just don't work. So, let's instead create an intention, an affirmation that is exciting, that is passion-driven, and that will be accomplished in ninety days. In other words, the subconscious can wrap its head around that. Let's say that we are a size twenty dress, and we want to be a size ten, and so we say to ourselves, "On or before ninety days from today, I am now wearing a size sixteen dress by doing the exercises necessary on a daily basis and eating a very clean diet." Now, if you go from a size twenty to a size sixteen, you are going to feel pretty darn good about yourself, and that is what we want your intentions or affirmations to be based on.

Here is a video I created on developing affirmations that may help: http://davidessel.com/life-relationship-business-coach

These affirmations or intentions will be stated at least two times every day; in the morning, the first thing when you wake up, and in the evening, right before you go to bed. The key is to repeat these affirmations or intentions with emotion and see that end result in your mind. So, if we look at sobriety, we would begin it with something like, "I am in the process of becoming a sober, happy, healthy person, attending events free of the need of alcohol, on or before...," or "I am an alcoholic and will ask for help on this date," and we would state the date. If it is a loving relationship, "I am in the process of forgiving my husband/wife/boyfriend/girlfriend for events that have occurred in the past. I am holding them in love, moving forward in our relationship every day between now and...," and say the date. In other words, whatever your "one thing" is, whatever your one goal is, if it is financial, if it is forgiveness, if it is sobriety, if it is walking your path with God, whatever the one thing is, we want that to be the focal point of your intention.

Do not make the mistake of saying, "I am sober; I am a millionaire; I am a size 8..." when you are not there yet! The subconscious mind will not buy into this, and within a short period of time you will revert back to old behaviors. Stop the fantastical thinking – it's time to get real.

Cancel Your Negative Thoughts

This brings me to the area of canceling out negative thoughts. All of us, on our path to greatness, will have thoughts of insecurity, jealously, resentment, or doubt, and those thoughts are okay. They may often arise in the beginning, especially around your one thing. You may be working on money issues, and even though you are doing all of this work, you are not seeing your income increase. You can fall into doubt. So, as you fall into doubt, and those thoughts come up saying, "I don't have the money I wanted to. I have been working really hard. Money is hard to create." Right away, say the word CANCEL, and then restate your affirmation, "I am in the process daily of doing the work necessary to increase my income by one thousand dollars a month on or before...," and state the ninety-day time period. In other words, we want to attack the negative thought process with the word CANCEL, and follow that thought process with the positive affirmation or intention you desire. This step is so important because we are retraining the brain, but, and I say this as a major warning, if you are trying to feed the brain nonsense, like, "I am a size two," when you are actually a size twenty, or, "I am earning one hundred thousand dollars a year," when you are only earning twenty thousand dollars a year, or, "I own five homes around the world," when you are renting a one-bedroom apartment... Whatever the fantasy intentions are, they are automatically thrown out by the subconscious. Over time these fantasy statements detract from our energy to do the work necessary on a daily basis.

The Second Key : Gratitude in a Different Way

The second key to manifestation are statements of gratitude. Now, we are going to approach the gratitude statements a little differently too. I do struggle with gratitude statements such as, "I am grateful for my new income of one hundred thousand dollars a year," when you are only earning twenty thousand dollars a year. I don't see them as productive. Once again, just like going back to the intention or affirmation statements, I see this as the brain saying, "Why are you wasting our time having gratitude for all of this money, when you don't have it?" Instead, what we teach in our courses is, to create a gratitude statement from a totally different perspective. Let's get focused on what we have right now regarding your one thing, and have gratitude for it, even if it isn't perfect, even if it isn't exactly what you want. So, we might say, "I have intense gratitude for my body, right now; my ability to walk and to see. Period." "I have gratitude for the money I am earning right now. Period." "I have gratitude for the home I am in, and that I have shelter and food. Period." In other words, as Eckhart Tolle stated so eloquently in his book "The Power of Now," everything is happening only in this present moment.

Miracles happen in the present moment, which means that if we want to exceed our own expectations, we better be appreciative of what we have right now, grounded, happy, healthy, even though it may not be ideal. If we can be happy now for our body, our money, our relationship, even for the struggles that we have, we will be exceptionally happy when life changes. But if we are living in denial, and we want to make up statements that are not true, that means that we are living in the future, and we cannot change the future. But if we have gratitude for the present, we can radically change the present.

The Third Key : Action Step into the Uncomfortable

The last step is the action step. This is step number three of the 3 Keys of Manifestation. How do you exceed your own expectations in life? It is all about action. We call this in our courses, the "seven-thousand-pound hammer for success," and it is really true. If people want to radically change their lives, it all comes down to action. Your mind is powerful, yes; your gratitude is powerful, yes, but nothing can reach the power of what you do on a daily basis to retrain the subconscious and to create success in your life. So, when you find your one major goal to go after, when you get highly focused and find your one thing, we recommend that you then create a system; five or even six days a week of action steps to bring you closer to your goal. If it is about money, your action steps could be tracking your income, or tracking your expenses. Your action steps could be increasing income or decreasing expenses. Your action steps could be decreasing debt. Five days a week in writing. These action steps must be specific, measurable, and time- lined. In other words, if you wanted to lose weight, Monday through Friday, from 6 a.m. in the morning until 7:30 a.m. in the morning, you are going to walk. So, here we have a specific, measurable, and time-lined action. We know the exact activity we are going to do; we know the exact time of day we are going to do it, and we know the exact length of time we are going to do it for. Specific, measurable, and time-lined. If it comes to forgiving someone, or maybe forgiving yourself, you might say, five days a week you are going to write letters of forgiveness to your partner or to yourself, or to someone who abused you in the past. Five days a week, you are going to write letters of anger, or angst, or jealously, or insecurity, to get those emotions out of us, and then follow that up once again with letters of forgiveness. In other words, the action steps are the key to life change. These letters are for your own benefit, never to be sent to the person you are writing about.

Over time, the action steps will change your belief systems. We do not believe that thinking positive thoughts has a long-term effect on changing your beliefs about being worthy of money, or love, or a better body, or a better job. We just don't believe that it has that power long-term. We believe positive thinking is crucial and important; an inevitable part of someone becoming more successful in life. We believe and have seen, in our work of thirty years, that people change their beliefs about themselves by being willing to do the action steps that are often uncomfortable five to six days per week.

Daily action is what changes belief systems, and that is what is going to help you to exceed your own expectations in life.

There is also something that we call "umbrella goals" that I am going to discuss briefly right now. I know a lot of people love to have those goals that say, "I am earning a million dollars a year," or "I own seven homes around the world." These are the goals that I'm not a huge fan of, but I know a lot of people are. Let's put these big goals underneath the category of "umbrella goals." If I'm working with someone who wants to exceed their expectations in life, I will say to them, "If you want to write an umbrella goal, go ahead." Let's say they are earning twenty thousand dollars a year, and they want to earn one hundred thousand dollars a year. In their writing, they will put down, "I am earning in twelve months, or twenty-four months, one hundred thousand dollars per year." I will have them write that down in a time frame that is realistic, and then put that away. Now, let's put our focus on our ninety-day goals and watch the umbrella goal become a reality down the road.

Morning Routines and Rituals

The next incredibly important topic I want to share with you is the most powerful way to start and end every day. In a focused approach to life, these two periods of our daily existence have been shown to be the two most important times of the day. For many of us, this is going to call for us to begin living our lives in a radically different way. So, here we go.

Morning routines. We need thirty minutes every morning to apply this new practice of focus. Plan on getting up thirty minutes earlier every day and find a space in your home that is quiet. Your computer can wait. The e-mails, texts and phone messages can wait. Some clients will say, "David, I already get up at 5 a.m. I couldn't imagine getting up any earlier!" But, with our highly focused approach to life, this is an incredibly crucial step to take in order to bring into your existence what you truly desire. Sit in a comfortable chair. Light a candle, and even incense, in order to set the mood for our new morning ritual.

Now, grab your coffee, your tea, or juice, and sit. Watch the candle, or if you're at a window, stare at the outside world. If you do have a window, or you have a balcony, put a birdfeeder up, or if you have a backyard, you could sprinkle birdfeed in the yard. Bring in the abundance of wildlife, the energy of wildlife. Bring in the energy of candles and incense. You might even have statues of religious figures or saints that you look at. Some people will make an altar. Some people, on this altar or in a corner of a room, will put their favorite paintings, or their favorite color. If you can, get a small tabletop water fountain to have on during this time of day as well.

Now, earlier in the book, I said, "There are going to be areas of this system that right- brained people are going to love," This section is for all of you right-brainers. You will really enjoy the whole spiritual, energetic approach to living. The logical left-brained people reading this are probably shaking their heads and saying, "Not more of this pooh- pooh spiritual stuff." It is not pooh-pooh spiritual stuff. All of these steps that I am recommending right now to start your day with, allow you to begin it in a highly focused way. For the first five minutes, just pay attention to your surroundings. Get centered.

Have your coffee, or tea, or juice. Listen to the water. Look at the flames. Smell the incense. Look at the birds on the outside. In other words, we are getting focused in the present moment; which is crucial to the start of every day.

Next, with a small pad of paper, write down a couple of things that you did well the day before. It just might be one or two. It doesn't have to be complicated. Maybe you stuck with your exercise program, or chose not to yell at your children when you usually would have for something they did. Or maybe you stayed late at work to complete a project.

Then, underneath that, write something that you did yesterday that you would like to change. Maybe yesterday you said you were going to walk, but you didn't, so today you are going to walk twice as far. In other words, we want to follow a yin-yang approach. The very next thing I want you to do as you sit and breathe, is look at one major challenge that you have in your life. If you notice, this is all going along with The One Thing Theory™. What is the one major challenge that you have going on that you are focused on, that you need answers for? Jot that down. It might be losing weight, making more money, or forgiving someone. It might be sticking with a spiritual program. It might be finding time to volunteer in your community. Just write down the one thing that is most crucial for you to figure out a way to accomplish today. Then just ask for help; you might be asking the internal self, you might be asking God, or you might be asking your guides around you. Just ask for help to solve this problem, to find the motivation to complete this task today. Whatever your greatest challenge is, do that. Then, put your pad down and just focus on your breathing. Continue to ask for guidance. During this thirty-minute period, periodically bring yourself back into the room. Look at the candle. Listen to the water. Look out the window. These thirty minutes of a highly-focused approach to starting your day will offer benefits far beyond anything that you might imagine.

The very last thing to do before you end this thirty minutes of solitude and focus in the morning, and this is where we get to have some fun, is to see, with a vibrant vision or feeling in your body, the end result of the life you desire. See yourself living in the mountains, or with an incredibly deep love relationship. See yourself at peace during times of challenge, or with a radically different body. See yourself sober, or maybe owning your own business. I want you to take the last five minutes of this thirty-minute period every morning, and immerse yourself in what you desire. As you can imagine, getting up from your chair after the contemplation, the focus, and then ending it with a vision of all that you desire, is going to be one of the most powerful ways to start the day. Just before you get up and leave, throw a thought out to the universe or a prayer that says, "And I ask you to bring this same feeling of success to everyone else in the world." Now you are ready to start your day in an extremely focused way. Within ninety days of following this morning system, you will automatically know that you are on a path of a high-focused approach to life, meaning that the end result will be that which you desire.

Evening Routine and Ritual

In the evening, we are going to have you end your day in a very similar way. Very simple. You can do this in bed. You can do it in a chair. Before you go to bed, grab your journal or a notebook, and just write down one or two things you did well that day. Just a couple of things that you say, "I am really proud of this." Again, we are going to re- encourage you to imprint in your brain that which is going well. Then write down one or two things that you have gratitude for. You might say, "I am really grateful that someone let me into traffic." "I am grateful that, I forgot my lunch and someone had extra food with them at work." Whatever you are grateful for. "I am grateful that my partner did not give me a hard time for tracking mud through the house." Whatever it is, just write a couple of statements of gratitude, and then you are ready for your rest.

Here is an example of a Morning Journal that may assist:

David Essel's

Daily Morning Journal Program

1) After relaxing with your coffee, tea or juice, make a list of a few things that you did the day before that you're very proud of. For example, maybe you completed your exercise program, or chose healthy foods or gave someone a compliment or even stayed late at work to complete a project. The idea here is to congratulate yourself for the 1,2,3 or maybe even 10 things that you did well. Complete this now and every day in the morning.

_____

_____

_____

_____

_____

_____

2) Now, below, list a few things that you did that you would like to change, correct, or do better today. For example maybe you didn't show the patience that you needed to with your children or coworker, or failed to complete your daily exercise program, or maybe you mentally berated yourself throughout the day for a mistake you made the week before. The purpose of this exercise is to put on paper those challenges that we are facing, that we would like to correct. When challenges are put on paper they become our reality, which means we are back in control. **You can then do things differently today, to get a different desired outcome.**

_____

_____

_____

_____

_____

_____

"David Essel is the New Leader of the "Positive Thinking Movement", I loved having him on my show, he opened up our eyes about the truth that's behind the reality of success!"

Jenny McCarthy, Radio Show Host, Actress, Author, TV Host

WWW.DAVIDESSEL.COM

You can download a printable version of this journal here: http://davidessel.com/wp-content/uploads/2016/08/DE-Morning-Journal-16.pdf

Chapter Review

Stop!

Now that you finished this chapter, it is very important that we slow down, and take a few minutes to answer the questions below.

Writing slows the brain down, and allows thoughts from the subconscious to come into consciousness, and this is one way we will take deep advantage of every chapter in this book.

Write. Right now. Let's keep moving towards our goals, with action steps such as these writing exercises, and not rely on our brain to create the life we desire anymore.

1. What was covered in detail, in this chapter?

_____

_____

_____

2. What was of most interest to you and why?

_____

_____

_____

3. What are 1 or 2 actions steps, relevant to the information in this chapter, that you could take right now to help you to focus more in life? Be specific, and also put the exact day and time that you will take these steps.

_____

_____

_____

Focus! Chapter 6:
Creating profound love, through focus

So, what is profound love? And what does it look like? For centuries people have written about love in so many different ways. Scientific journals. Love novels. Erotic novels. There's soulmate love. Arranged relationships. Arranged marriages. And in all of these instances, many people will have many different opinions about what profound love really is.

But with extreme focus, the kind of focus we are offering in this book, you can make up your mind about what level of profound love you would like to go to, the changes that you may have to make within your own life, and what you're willing or not willing to put up with in relationships from this moment forward.

To me, profound love is heartfelt love. It's intense love. It's great love. It's the kind of love that you rarely see, sad but true, profound love is not to be found on every corner.

In the past 28 years as a radio talk show host, I have interviewed so many couples in love, at least 100 experts in the world of relationships, and one of the things everyone has in common when we talk about profound love, is that it's a combination of several characteristics. Number one? Profound self-love, which I'll explain in a minute. Friendship. Lust. Desire. And a willingness to support each other during the great as well as the challenging times.

Now the above is a mouthful! If you reread everything that I have put on paper up to now in this chapter, you can do a self-evaluation. Do you understand profound love? Are you acting in ways that depict profound love and are you with someone who is on the same wavelength?

Self-Love

The only place to begin is with profound self-love. Heartfelt self-love. Intense self-love. Great self-love. And regardless of what you might be thinking right now, this is one of the rarest traits that a human being can ever acquire.

In order to love ourselves in profound ways, we must be free of all addictions. And right away, we probably knock out a huge percentage of the population. This statement is not a statement of judgment, simply fact. You cannot love yourself in a profound, deep way if you're addicted to food, nicotine, sex, alcohol, prescription or street drugs, emotional spending, workaholism, judgment, anger, resentment...... I think you get the picture.

And there are even more addictions that someone might have than what are listed above. But self-love is rare because most of us suffer with some type of an addiction or dependency in life.

So, guess what? The first step to profound love is to remove any dependency or Addiction that is getting in the way of you loving yourself in the most profound way possible. Your body is your temple. You can't claim that you love yourself completely, when you're damaging the temple that you carry around.

So here we are back to focus. This could very well be your one thing, the one thing that you have procrastinated, denied, delayed working on that we need to start attacking today. Without eliminating all addictions and dependencies, we cannot ever reach the deepest, most profound state of self-love.

We have to break through justification, rationalization and denial in order to see the truth, in order to change the truth, in order to move into self-love. But don't confuse this with perfection. There's a big difference between someone that has one drink on a Friday night, and someone who has 10 drinks on a Friday night.

There's a big difference between someone that has a piece of cake on Sunday afternoon, and someone who needs sugar seven days a week. Do you understand where I'm going? I'm not asking for perfection, but I am asking for extreme focus, that we take off the masks of denial, look in the mirror of reality, and make the changes necessary in order to say that we truly do love ourselves in the most profound way possible.

One of the greatest examples of someone who has acquired profound love is my friend Evelyn Keiling. I have interviewed Evelyn multiple times on my radio show, I've even done YouTube videos about the profound turn around in her life.

You see Evelyn Keiling to date has lost over 245 pounds! Imagine that. 245 pounds of weight loss and, she not only lost this huge amount of weight, but she's kept it off for a number of years. And let me take it a step further.

A little over a year ago, after losing all this weight and committing herself to an intense and beautiful exercise and eating program, Evelyn walked on stage in front of 15,000 screaming fans in Las Vegas as a body sculpting competitor. In her 50s!

Evelyn did not blame her weight gain on genetics. Evelyn did not blame her weight gain on anything other than her own choices. You see this is profound love. When you can look in the mirror, and accept responsibility for where you are in your life with your body, addictions, lack of confidence, lack of self-esteem, you are on your way to profound self-love. On the stage with Evelyn we're photos of her 245 pounds heavier. The crowd was going insane.

She is one of the most beautiful examples of someone who turned it around midlife, stopped making up excuses, stopped using justification, rationalization and denial and decided to do the hard work necessary day after day after day to create the body she always wanted, another sign of profound love.

And today her mission is to inspire millions of people around the world, and she's doing a damn great job doing so. What did it take on Evelyn's part to change her life so radically? Focus. Focus. Focus.

She did what we are guiding you to do in this book, she looked at the area of life that she had denied, delayed and procrastinated and went after it 110%. Her body is her temple now. It wasn't before, but it sure is now. She is one of the most wonderful, giving, compassionate women I have ever met and interviewed. I love her for who she is inside, and for the transformation she made in the outside world. All because of focus.

Remember, you can do the same thing. Follow the steps in this book, get accountability professionals to hold your feet to the fire, commit without excuses, to your new life change. And you can become the next Evelyn Keiling, regardless if you need to lose 25, 100, or 300 pounds. That's profound self-love.

Codependency Destroys Profound Love

In 2002 we claimed that "codependency is the largest Addiction in the world." And I believe it still is to this day. In order to be able to love ourselves profoundly, and then carry that on over to a relationship, we must shatter our codependent nature.
So, what is codependency? What is codependency in relationships? That's such a beautiful, deep and confusing question for many.

Codependency is a craving for love, craving for attention, a craving to be accepted, a craving to be noticed, a craving to be included.

It's a fear of rocking the boat. A fear of being rejected, judged, abandoned. Codependency is staying with a partner who refuses to get help for their addictions, mental conditions or anything else that's destroying the relationship.

Codependency can show up as victimhood, where we refuse to accept responsibility, for all the bad things that happen. It's always because of other people.

Codependency can come out in the form of the martyr, who constantly professes how they do everything for everyone else, while neglecting their own mental, physical, financial and spiritual needs.

As you can tell, codependency is absolutely huge. The codependent puts the desire to be liked by others, and all of the other traits I mentioned above, on steroids. Of course, it's natural to want to be included, admired, liked and even loved... But the codependent puts so much pressure on themselves and others that it turns into an addiction. Completely unhealthy.

If there's anyone in this world who has become an expert on codependency, because of their own mistakes in life, it is me. The guy writing this book. Up until 1997, if someone would've said that David Essel was an extreme codependent in relationships, I would've looked at them laughed and walked away. Why? Because in my mind, David Essel was the most independent man in this world.

But that wasn't true. In my intimate relationships, I had a very hard time expressing my emotions. If I was unhappy, I might make one or two stabs at saying something to my partner, but then I would shut down. I might use alcohol and or drugs and or work to escape the situation in regards to the person I was dating, instead of flat out looking for an answer to our issues.

Up until 1997 I would even go into the arena of having an affair, rather than facing the reality that my relationship is in trouble, dying or even dead. And then something magical happened that year. I was working with a counselor who I admired greatly, and asking her to help me out with my current relationship struggles. They had returned again. Within four weeks she looked at me and said, "David you are the most codependent man I have ever met."

I had no idea what she was talking about, even though I was a counselor and a life coach then, I couldn't understand how she was calling me codependent when I was such an independent person... In my own mind.

I committed the rest of that year to work on, and understand my own codependent nature. I hated to rock the boat. I hated conflict, I hated to confront problems when I could just as easily drink them away or walk away.

Through our work together, I found that I was staying in relationships far too long after they had expired. I found out my avoidance techniques were probably some of the most unhealthy ways to deal with love, that might seem logical to other people but not to the codependent. I never wanted to rock the boat, and I didn't want anyone else to rock the boat either. Extremely unrealistic, with a complete lack of focus.

Since that time, in my intimate relationships, I have slipped and returned to codependent ways, but I've caught them so fast that I rarely have experienced any serious damage from that time forward. I would never stray from an intimate relationship and have an affair ever again. I would never let a topic that was unsettling me inside stay unspoken from that day until today. And this is one of the reasons why 50% of my work in the world of counseling and life coaching happens to be in the area of codependency.

The codependent cannot experience profound self-love. It's impossible. It just doesn't work. As you can imagine, the codependent is all about avoiding, enabling, versus actually working in the arena of love.

The only way to shatter codependency is to be able to write about the patterns of how codependent you have been in your life. Look back at all of your relationships, with extreme focus, and see where your codependent nature has created hell on earth in your intimate relationships and maybe even your friendships and relationships with family members.

Most of our codependent nature is handed down by society as well as role models in childhood. So, you must look closely to see where it began, and how you have repeated it in order to shatter it.

The first time that I ran into independent people that I can remember was when I was a freshman at Syracuse University in 1974. I came from a very codependent lifestyle, codependent high school where 80% of the girls if you asked them out would say yes, because they didn't want to hurt anyone's feelings. See, that's codependency.

But my world was about to be shattered by a girl from New York City who I was very attracted to my freshman year in college. My best friend Jake and I had gone to a party in a dormitory when my eyes connected on this gorgeous woman. Even though I played on the Syracuse University basketball team, I was shy in nature. I was never an extrovert in life unless alcohol was involved. Well guess what, alcohol was involved.

So, I went over to her and started talking to her, and she reacted quite beautifully. We were laughing, joking around and then before I walked away I said "you know what I would really love to get together with you. I think we could have a great time, so how about tomorrow night?"

She looked at me, hesitated, and said "no not interested at all. But have a great night." I couldn't believe it! Rejected by a woman? Are you kidding me? I walked away thinking to myself what a bitch. I talked to Jake about it, and he laughed and concluded the same thing. I had not realized that men and women who speak honestly with what is on their mind are actually independent in nature. Instead? I took it as an insult.

Years later I laugh as I recall that story because she was an incredibly independent woman. She had no interest in me, and she wasn't going to play any games. That's who I want you to become. You can do it with love, compassion, and empathy but you must speak openly and honestly if you want to see profound self-love in your own life. If you want to become that beautiful, independent person you are meant to be. Focus. Focus. Focus.

Here are two videos I think you'll enjoy and codependency:

Number one. Codependency: the largest silent Addiction in the world at www.davidessel.com/co-dependency-kills/

Number two. Codependency with alcohol, food and low self-esteem at www.davidessel.com/holistic-addiction-recovery/

Radical Forgiveness

The next step to create profound self-love, is to forgive ourselves for anything that we've done in the past that is incorrect. Think about it, people who forgive themselves carry no shame or guilt from the past, but rather realize their errors and make amends with themselves in order to move forward with self-confidence and self-esteem.

So, what do you need to forgive yourself for? Cheating on someone? Stealing money from someone? Gossiping about others? Cheating on tests? Lying to your partner? Lying to your best friend? Are you a fraud on social media, making statements about how perfect, successful or loving you are when in reality you're none of those things?

Work with a counselor or a life coach in order to find the path of work for you in order to forgive yourself for anything that you've done inappropriately from childhood to today. People with self-love do not live with shame and or guilt. They take care of it. They do the hard work, through focus, in order to be free of their past, clear in the present and ready to love in the future. Focus, once again it's all about focus.

After you forgive yourself for the errors you've made in life, whether you want to or not you're going to have to forgive everyone else who has ever hurt you, betrayed you, or lied to you if you want to be able to experience profound self-love.

Resentments at others rob us of energy, compassion, creativity and yes self-love. When we hear someone else's name who cheated on us 30 years ago, and our stomach boils, that's a sign that you haven't done the work and you need to do it now. We forgive others not for their sake, but to release the poison that resides within us.

I have had to do this work with counselors to first forgive myself for the ways I've treated other people inappropriately, and then also to forgive others who have done something similar to me.

One of the most profound areas of forgiving others that I've experienced had to do with a woman I dated a number of years ago who treated me with extreme disrespect and betrayal. At one point I said to myself that I would never forgive her for the rest of my life. I couldn't imagine letting her off the hook after the way that she had repeatedly mistreated me in life.

Then one day, after a session in which I had helped a woman to forgive someone who had beaten her, and looking at the success in her eyes after being free of her own resentments at them, I decided it was time for me to do work on myself. So that day I began writing. It took me eight months of writing on a daily basis to get to the space of forgiveness. That might seem like a long time, but there can be a lot of submerged pain when you've been with someone who has betrayed you.

So, after eight months of writing letters about my anger and disgust with the way she treated me, of course we never send them to anyone, my heart began to open up. Then I began writing letters of forgiveness to her, once again that will never be sent, to see if I truly had forgiven her.

After that, I wrote letters to myself forgiving myself for holding onto the resentments as long as I did. She was not being negatively affected by my anger, rage and resentment... Only I was. So, writing those letters were a huge benefit for me.

This was a person who I loved very deeply. She had borrowed a huge amount of money from me for various reasons. We had agreed in a written contract that she would pay the money back. After the relationship ended she texted me one day and said "after speaking to my mom and several girlfriends I don't owe you a penny. You did what boyfriends do. You're supposed to support me by giving me money, so I'm not paying you back."

I was not only in shock, I was infuriated. How could someone do this? How could someone sleep at night when they treated someone so incredibly poorly? When they betrayed someone? When they borrow a large amount of money and walk away, with no intention of repaying it? When they lied to them?

And that is the justification, for holding onto my resentment. But here's the greatest news in the world. After doing all this work on forgiving her, and forgiving myself for even staying in the relationship, I became free. I had to accept the fact that even when I saw a red flag waving in the wind about not being able to trust her, I continued to loan her money. It didn't matter if we had written agreements. I should've seen the chaos coming, but I chose not to. That is my error. And I had to own it, and forgive myself, in order to move on.

And then I started to write with compassion and empathy as to why she did what she did. And when I looked at her background, the way she was raised, she was just repeating what she learned in childhood. Her role models were obviously terrible, and she was just living life on the terms that were given to her as a child. Entitled. Self-centered. Sad, but true, we often become our parents.

Now, this does not excuse her behavior, but it allowed me after doing a lot of work, to let all of this go, to have empathy and compassion, and to create a new existence.

Just before a massive hurricane hit our area, I reached out to her to make sure her and her children were OK. I had broken through my own anger, rage and resentment, and wanted just to make sure that they had a safe place to go during the storm.

She responded back and thanked me for reaching out. We communicated a few times, and of course because I'm a counselor, she leaned on me for advice as she was in a difficult relationship. I had no problem helping her via phone and text, and that also proved that my forgiveness was real.

But like I tell all my clients, just because you forgive someone doesn't mean they have to be a part of your life. I don't think this person will ever be an intimate part of my life, because from the very last day I saw her until today, she has made no serious attempts to own her responsibility for the money stolen, or the various forms of betrayal that she did. And I honestly don't need it. Now if I wanted her to be back into my close circle of friends, she would have to prove she was serious in order to be welcomed back into my life. But I doubt she'll ever want that, and I don't need it, so I can forgive her and feel 100% free, which is the exact opposite of the way I was living for a period of time. If she texted me today and asked for help with her children or a new relationship... I would of course help her. It's what I do, and I'm fine with it. You have to make a decision on how you want to treat people who have betrayed you in the past, but the most important thing is to get the poison out of your heart and soul.

Notice that I am not a victim here, and I don't encourage anyone to pull the victim mentality when you've been betrayed. Forgiveness means you've got to move on, it also means you never forget the experience you had with a particular person or persons. I often put on Facebook "if you pick up a rattlesnake and it bites you, don't be surprised if you pick it up again and your bitten again. The same is true in regards to people who have betrayed you in the past." Think about it.

It takes extreme focus, hard work, in order to forgive people that have hurt us, and it is one of the deepest signs of self-love that you could ever experience.

I have helped people who have been brutally raped to forgive their rapist. I've helped people who were sexually molested by their own mothers or fathers to forgive those individuals as well. I have helped individuals whose children have been murdered, or who died unexpectedly learn how to go through the grieving process to forgive themselves, anyone else involved, and even God. This is a form of profound self-love.

Am I emotionally available for deep and profound love?

Take this short quiz below and let's see where you rate regarding being emotionally available for profound love:

One. Is my pattern in dating and marriage one poor choice after another?

Two. Do I shut down when my needs are not being met or act out in anger, Addiction or passive aggressive behavior?

Number three. Do I regularly date people with addictions or dependencies to alcohol, smoking, food, sex, work, shopping or who are codependent with their families, friends or children?

Number four. Am I afraid to set boundaries with consequences when my partner does or says things that are harmful or inappropriate?

Number five. Do I date people who are separated but not divorced?

If you answered yes to any of the above questions, there's a very great chance that you are emotionally unavailable in love. The good news? If we want to get focused and do the work, we can change this pattern forever

But it's going to take time, effort, and discipline on your part to shatter these behaviors that have been a part of who we are for many years.

Kate came in to work with me after a string of terrible relationships and marriages. When we went back into her childhood, her dad was never there for her emotionally and or physically. She was a bother to him. A pest. And because of that, she was attracted to the only type of man she ever knew: emotionally unavailable men. She was repeating the pattern from childhood, and wanted to shatter it. With extreme focus, today, she is becoming a radically different person.

Recently, she was approached by an acquaintance who had sent her in an erotic love letter, and she was the star of the letter. In the past she told me that any type of attention from men was better than none, and she would've acted out and met him immediately in order to feel the affection and attention from a man. She shared that this would've led to sex, probably on that very same night, and she's had enough of being trapped in relationships with emotionally unavailable men. Her answer this time? A big, fat, no.

Nancy was attracted to men who were addicts, alcoholics and abusive. When we started working together she had no idea the pattern was so strongly set in her past, but through the writing exercises it became apparent to her that there was not one man she ever dated who was emotionally available. Where did all this come from? Her father was a tyrant growing up. He showed no respect for her mother. So, whether we want to think that our childhood has very little bearing on our role as an adult, that's not true at all. She saw within four months of working together that she was dating men just like her father. She is now taking a year off from dating, and her sense of profound self-love is rising to the surface every day.

Thomas continually fell in love with women who were separated or just recently out of long-term relationships. He came in very frustrated, because every relationship that he was in ended the same way... The woman eventually would walk away because he was too needy for their liking. The reality is, Thomas was not emotionally available himself, and was consistently attracted to women who were not emotionally available either. Six months after working together, and choosing not to date in that period of time, he saw the writing on the wall and started to get involved with women who were emotionally and physically available. The lightbulb went off through his intense focus, and he is a completely changed man today.

Elise came to me wondering why her relationships were filled with complete chaos and drama. Again, with intense focus in the writing exercises I gave her, she came in one day with her mouth basically dropped open to the floor. "David, I can't believe the pattern here... I'm going after men with money, and most of them have no interest in a serious relationship."

When I asked her to do additional homework on why she wanted to only go after them men with money, it became apparent that this was from her childhood as well. "My mom told me ever since I was a little girl, that the only good man to marry is one who has a lot of money so I don't have to work. My mom hated men, and only wanted to use them for whatever she could get out of them. I picked up that message as a very young girl, and even though I'm in my late 40s today, David I am still playing that role. Her voice is still in my head."

Elise is trying to figure out right now as I write this book, if she wants to take off time from the world of dating in order to change this belief system about using men for their money. She is struggling. And I understand why. When we are given messages as young individuals, from the age of 0 to 18, about what love looks like, or what love should look like according to our parents, it gets stuck in the subconscious mind and many times it's very difficult to remove. Not impossible. As a matter of fact, through with the exercises I'm giving you here, if we focus and do the work, we can shatter any belief system whatsoever that is not serving us today. One of the most important tips to remember in the world of dating, is that if we are attracting unavailable man and or women it is a direct sign that we are emotionally unavailable as well. And I know that's a hard pill to swallow.

A healthy, independent man or woman, would be able to sniff out any emotionally unavailable potential partner within the first 90 days of dating if not sooner. When we are emotionally available, we would never even walk into a love relationship with someone who is separated, or married. We would never stay with someone who is emotionally abusive, or physically abusive. We would never stay with someone who drank too much, or disrespected their body or their money. We just wouldn't be able to stay in that energy.

As you focus with the information in this book, I promise you your life will radically change. Will it be difficult? Will it take a lot of effort? Will it take a total change in the way you approach the world of love and self-love? Absolutely! And it will be damn worth it.

The World of Dating

Speaking of the world of dating, we have an incredible tool that we created 20 years ago to help people get serious about shattering their negative and limiting belief systems regarding the world of dating.

As a matter of fact, my friend and celebrity Jenny McCarthy absolutely loves the next two tips I'm going to give you when it comes to creating profound self-love and love with another.

The first one is called "David Essel's 3% rule of dating"™. What this rule basically says is, you can have 97% compatibility with someone but if they have any of your 3% deal killers in love, the relationship will never work. Never. Ever. Ever.

When I have my clients do this simple exercise, they write down all the deal killers in love. I ask them to look at their past relationships, and the traits that the people had that were not healthy for them and create a complete list, and once the list is created never to allow these to enter your world of dating.

So, here's what your list of deal killers in love might look like, but you'll have to create your own in the space below:

"I could never date... A smoker, someone who is separated or married, someone with young children, someone who doesn't want children, a Republican, Democrat, someone who doesn't exercise, someone who's addicted to sports, or any addiction whatsoever, a workaholic, a gossiper, someone who puts others down on a regular basis..."

Do you get the idea? Now the above examples are just a starting point, but you should know by now if you're over the age of 25 what works for you and doesn't work for you in love.

The big problem that I've seen with so many people in the world of dating, is that they might create the list above, and then break their own rules. So, take a moment right now and in the lines following write out what your deal killers in love are, the traits that you know from this moment forward, would never work for you:

_____

_____

_____

_____

_____

_____

Remember, if you want profound love you must be able to respect yourself. If you end up breaking your own "deal breakers in love "list, expect nothing less than chaos and drama in your life.

Here's a video I think you'll like on our 3% rule of dating at www.davidessel.com/love-relationships-10-hour-course/

You can have 97% compatibility, let me repeat this, you can have 97% compatibility with someone but if they're carrying one of your deal breakers and they choose not to change it, the relationship will eventually crash and burn. You can always ask someone if they would be willing to change, and as long as they're doing it for themselves and you that's fine. But if someone tells you that they'll stop drinking or smoking in order to be with you, and if you see they're carrying resentments for this choice, you will have to be the one strong enough to walk away.

The Love Scale: 1 - 10

The last item, and Jenny McCarthy loves this one as well, that I want to discuss with you regarding creating profound self-love as well as profound love with another is something that once again we came up with over 20 years ago called "David Essel's love scale: 1 to 10"™.

The love scale is used to explain what is healthy love and what is unhealthy love in an incredibly specific way. This approach to explaining love came about 22 years ago, when a young woman came into work with me and couldn't understand why her relationship was filled with so much chaos and drama, when she loved the man she was with more than anyone else she had ever loved in her life.

She couldn't understand why he was always so angry at her. Always upset with her. As our work continued, the answers came to the surface quite readily.

She couldn't follow her words in love. She would be the shining star in his eyes for three days and then she would completely reverse her actions and become A nightmare for him.

As she started to open up, it was evident that she was on the lower end of the love scale that I'm about to explain in a minute. She was self-sabotaging her own relationship. When she started giving me examples of why he was so upset, it became apparent that she was modeling love from her childhood in the most unhealthiest of ways.

There will be days that she would promise her boyfriend that she would pick up the dry cleaning for him because he was so busy, and then never do it. He would ask her on a date to a movie, and she would show up 20 minutes late when she had nothing else to do the entire day. She sat in my office with eyes as big as a deer in headlights, totally surprised that he would be this upset with her day after day after day.

As I went into her childhood with her the answers became quite apparent. She was raised in an extremely dysfunctional household, emotionally and physically abused as a child, and did not trust men at all. Because she had never done the work to release the damage done in her childhood, she would only be able to hold it together in respectful ways with her boyfriend for a few days, before the subconscious mind would kick in and she would act in the exact opposite way then she had promised him she would.

When he came into the office, I saw total exasperation. They had been together about four months, and he was at the end of his rope. I explained to both of them the scale of love, because he looked at me and said, "how the hell can she say she loves me more than any other man in life, and constantly betray me and disrespect me?"

It's a great question. Here's the answer. We put love on a scale of 1 to 10. The lower levels of love, numbers one through four, are still love but it's highly dysfunctional love. Let me explain them right now. The love scale 1 to 10:

Number one. Physical abuse, addiction, emotional abuse. Most people who are here are individuals who have been abused in childhood. Neglected. This is the only love they've ever known, so they share it with others in a way that was shared with them. When I work with women who have been physically abused, and they want to return once again to the relationship, they will say the same thing that my client said above "but we love each other, I love him more than anyone I've ever loved." It's love, in the form of toxicity.

Number two. Emotional abuse, betrayal, Addiction. Once again, a child's upbringing has everything to do with our perception of love.

Number three. Lies, manipulative behavior, affairs... This is the world of people who love at this level.

Number four. Passive aggressive behavior, extreme codependency, neediness, enabling.

Number five. This is the where the stage of healthy love begins, here is where friendship is. Respect.

Number six. Friendship, plus passion lies here.

Number seven. Friendship, passion, and a mutual desire for both people to win in the relationship and in life.

Number eight. Enthusiasm for our partner to succeed, even if it means we never reach the level that they do professionally, or personally. High levels of extreme interest, passion, understanding.

Number nine. Take numbers five through eight, and you have number nine. It's an amazing, compassionate, sympathetic, empathetic relationship where life is lived at the highest level in every area.

Number 10. Unconditional love. OK this is a tricky one. I know so many books and people talk about unconditional love, but I have yet to honestly see it very often at all in 28 years of relationship counseling, other than my parents and a few other people that I honestly believe exhibit unconditional love with their partners.

It's more common to see unconditional love between parents and their children then it is to see unconditional love between two adults. It's more common to see unconditional love between dog owners and their pets, then it is to see it amongst people. It doesn't mean it doesn't exist, but it's extremely rare.

I see too many people who claim they love someone unconditionally, when really it's just the highest form of codependency possible. It's enabling. I remember once working with someone who loved her husband so much, who was a complete alcoholic, with no care in the world about anything other than having his needs met, even at her demise. She tried to explain to me that that's what unconditional love looks like, but I could not agree. She was a nervous wreck, on anti-anxiety and anti-depression medication, she was a martyr. It was one of the most unhealthiest love relationships I had ever seen, but she had been convinced by books and organizations that she loved her husband unconditionally. I just don't see it.

Now remember, if you're looking at this list and you say oh my Lord my partner is a one, or two, or three, or four... I'm going to tell you something that you may not want to hear. The only way you can continue to return to an unhealthy love relationship that would be numbers 1 to 4 on the scale, would be if you were at their same level in one way or another. Maybe you're just extremely codependent. Maybe you have no boundaries in love. So, it doesn't mean if you're with a 2 who emotionally abuses you that you're an emotional abuser, but it does mean that if you stay with that person that you cannot be above them on the scale of 1 to 10. Does that make sense?

Here is a video that I think you might like on our love scale at www.davidessel.com/love-relationships-10-hour-course/

With focus, you can look at the scale if you're single and choose to only be with people from number five to number 10. If you're in a relationship, you can look at the scale and make a decision to get in and work with a counselor or a coach starting today, if you notice that you and or your partner are below number five. Don't wait. Focus, and act today.

What does Profound Love Look Like?

I'd like to end this chapter with a few different examples of what profound love has looked like in my work over the years:

Number one. OK I admit it, I've got to talk about my mom and dad. I'm not sure if they are at a 10, of unconditional love, but I guarantee you they are at a nine. They are each other's best friends. I've seen them negotiate through some very difficult times, my dad's depression after he lost his job when we're young kids, and how they negotiated financial challenges over and over and over again.

I believe, that the number one reason that they have had such a very long, 67-year healthy marriage, is because they put so much faith in God. This doesn't mean you have to, but it works for them. They have compromised repeatedly. I have never heard my dad put my mom down ever, or my mom put my dad down in public. They have teased each other about the way they drive etc., but they have the utmost of respect and love for each other.

I've seen compromise over and over again. My mom is a huge animal freak, we have had every kind of pet imaginable from birds, to lizards, to fish, to dogs... And my dad is not an animal lover at all. I smile as I write this, because he was just never raised around animals. My mom was, and she wanted them all the time in our lives. My dad went along with it, never complained that much at all, LOL, but he supported my mom in this way more than I've seen anyone else do it in my life.

I've worked with hundreds of couples over the last 28 years where there's been an affair, but the one couple that stands out the most I love to talk about all the time. When I met them, they were married about 15 years, and the last four years of their marriage had slowly started to go downhill.

Which led, to the affair. But after the affair, I worked with them both for 12 straight months individually, and they reclaimed a level of love and respect you rarely ever see in life. Constantly holding each other's hands, he holds every door open for her imaginable, and she looks at him when he does that and gives him a kiss on the cheek and says thank you. It's beautiful. And now I've never been in the bedroom with them together, of course, but they have reported to me that their love life after doing the work, and focusing on forgiveness, is more sensual and real then they could've ever imagined. And now they've been married over 27 years. To have a vibrant intimate, sexual life after being married for over 27 years is an absolute beautiful thing to share.

And the last story, is another beautiful one as well, is about two people who profoundly love each other. The husband came to me after a 30-year battle with opiate addiction that he could never quite beat. Until now. His wife had given him an ultimatum that this was it, he had relapsed one too many times, and if he didn't get his act together the marriage is over.

He came in to work with me on his addiction humble, open, honest and real. And man, did we kick butt together. Within 12 weeks he was completely clean, he had done everything I had asked him to do plus, and his life was radically turning around.

Months down the road I get a phone call from his wife, which at first scared me. Normally when I get those calls, it's because their partner had relapsed. But this, was a totally different call. As she was talking to me on the phone tears were streaming down both her face and my face as she said "David, I've never seen the man who I'm living with in 30 years. I have never seen the compassion, empathy, sympathy, and attention that I'm seeing from my husband today. Do you know that he leaves me love notes every morning? Do you know that he is scheduled vacations for us for the next four years? Do you know that when we're making love for the first time in our lives he looks me directly in the eyes and tells me he loves me? He has become the man I always knew we could be, I don't know if it's unconditional love, but if it's not, it's very close to it."

Now I will tell you, the three examples above are also examples of extreme focus. Profound love is possible, when you look to serve your partner. When you take care of your own inconsistencies. When you look at compromise as a win, versus a compromise. When you start to take time out of your day to let your partner know you're thinking of them. When you forgive them, because they're doing the work too, for any transgressions in the past.

It takes a hell of a lot of hard work, an amazing amount of focus, humility and vulnerability to get to the level of love that these people have reached. I want that for you. I want you to look in your partners eyes when you're making love and create the most profound unity that you could ever imagine. I want to hear about the thrill coming from your partner when you surprise them with a small gift on a weekly basis.

I want to hear about the change in your life, when you clean up your own addictions and dependencies and take all that time that you've put into those areas of life into your partner. I want your children to see the most amazing example of profound love between you and your partner, so that they have the role models they need to be able to repeat that in their lives.

And I know, without a moment of hesitation, that if you focus on the steps that we are giving in this book that you can create profound love with yourself and another. You have to want it bad enough, to make the changes inside yourself first, and once you do, look out world! Love will surround you. Honesty will be your middle name. Service will be effortless, for the ones you love.

Chapter Review

Stop!

Now that you finished this chapter, it is very important that we slow down, and take a few minutes to answer the questions below.

Writing slows the brain down, and allows thoughts from the subconscious to come into consciousness, and this is one way we will take deep advantage of every chapter in this book.

Write. Right now. Let's keep moving towards our goals, with action steps such as these writing exercises, and not rely on our brain to create the life we desire anymore.

1.   What was covered in detail, in this chapter?

_____

_____

_____

2.   What was of most interest to you and why?

_____

_____

_____

3. What are 1 or 2 actions steps, relevant to the information in this chapter, that you could take right now to help you to focus more in life? Be specific, and also put the exact day and time that you will take these steps.

_____

_____

_____

Focus! Chapter 7:
Karma: Enhance it With Daily Focus

"You are worthy of every goal you desire."

Karma is a passionate topic of mine. When it comes to getting highly focused in life, one of the most important things we need to realize, and learn, and understand, is the whole definition of karma. What is it? What is this karma? People talk about it all of the time, right? You reap what you sow. What goes around comes around. All of those statements or definitions of karma are true, but I want to take it to even a deeper level, because if we start to really focus on what the true meaning of karma is, we will be able to radically change our lives and make healthier decisions daily, which will bring a different end result to our life. And in this chapter, we will explore two totally different depictions of karma. Buckle up, they might surprise you.

Let's go back again to 1996. It was a magical year for me. I remember my very first coaching client that I trained to be a life coach. During the very last part of the course, which I still teach identically today, we went over what is called the "ripple effect." The ripple effect is karma. The definition that I used back then, we still use today: "Every thought, every word, and every action that you do or have goes out into the universe and returns in kind." Reread that statement. This is one of the most powerful understandings of the way life works. If we can grasp its meaning, it will help us make totally different decisions on a day-to-day basis, maybe even a minute-to-minute basis, ultimately helping us to exceed our own expectations and create the life that we totally desire and deserve.

Think about it. This is powerful. Every thought, every word, and every action you have is going out into the universe and returning in kind. Thoughts of judgment like, "They are so lucky that they have all of that money." "They are so lucky with their genetics that they don't have to work out to have that beautiful body." "They have it made, and I don't." However, we are judging the world, we are judging ourselves. When we put that negative energy out by judging other people, that negative energy is coming back.

Sometimes it comes back by other people judging us and saying unkind things to us, but sometimes it comes back just within our own internal lack of self-confidence. You can imagine, that if you stopped judging others, you would stop judging yourself. You would have more energy, be more creative, and be more in love with yourself now and always. What an amazing way to focus your energy. There is no more diversion with our thoughts. Now this takes focus. I admit that initially, it takes a lot of focus to be highly aware that our thoughts, our words, and our actions go out into the universe and come back to us in kind. It means we have to be on top of our game, which is what this book is all about; helping you to get focused.

We want for you to awaken and say, "The reason why I am struggling with finances is the fact that I haven't always been honest with my tax returns." This is true. Sometimes people, during our work together, will wonder, "Why am I always struggling financially?" "Why am I always struggling in love?" "Why am I always struggling in..." whatever it might be. We will look at karma. Let's take your money. I might ask, "In the last ten or fifteen years, have you not reported all of your income to the IRS?" They will look at me and say, "Well, yeah. I don't want to report it all." I will say, "Have you embellished any of your expenses?" "In other words, do you take your family out to dinner and write it off as an expense?" "Well, yeah, but everyone does that." We will get through this whole list, and all of a sudden at the end of it, they will look at me and say, "Oh my Lord! It is karma, isn't it? In other words, I am struggling financially because I'm not honest in my financial life." Bingo! Lights go off. Now, the cool thing is, we can change that. Someone else might be struggling in love. They might be in a relationship, where they are always bickering, always arguing. Then they realize through these exercises that they're constantly gossiping about their lover to their family or to their friends. They're constantly thinking negative thoughts that "he or she isn't living up to my expectations," or "he or she is doing that again." And all of a sudden it dawns on them, "Our relationship is in total hell because of the fact that I am constantly talking about my partner in negative ways." Well, the thoughts, words, and actions go out into the world, and they come back to us, right? So, karma is simple. It is easy to understand. And, the best news, it is reversible.

So, how do we reverse karma? How do we actually take what is not going well with our life, find the starting point and change it?

First, let's take a look at the concept of karma in this brief video: http://davidessel.com/deepen-your-spiritual-path-now-10-hour-course

Now, grab a piece of paper, or a small notebook, and every time you judge yourself or someone else, just put an X down. You might judge someone who is a terrible driver in traffic. Just put an X. You might judge yourself as you look in the mirror and say, "You've gained more weight." Just put down an X. You might look at a woman with an incredible body and lots of jewelry, and say, "She's such a snob." Put an X down. If someone mentions something about the administration, the President of the United States, our economy, or whatever it might be, and you add your two cents, you are a part of the gossip. Put an X down. I think you get the point here.

When we start to see how often our mind is wrapped in

negativity, our words are wrapped in gossip, or our actions are not as loving and kind as they need to be, we can then get a grasp of where our karma is coming from.

The next thing we need to do is to forgive ourselves. So, step number one is to get an idea of how many times a day all of these negative thoughts, and words, and actions are going on. Step number two, at the end of every day, just write a statement, or you could even mentally say, "I forgive myself for all thoughts, words, and actions that were unkind today." Cancel these out, bringing in only words, thoughts, and actions that are kind and life-supporting. Period.

Next, you've got to change your actions. Forgive yourself for what you've done, then we need to be looking for ways to help others in order to reverse our karma. There are many awesome books that talk about this in great detail. One that comes to mind is called "Karmic Management." The more that we ask others, "How can I help you?", the more we look for ways to help others daily, the faster we reverse our negative old karma and supplant it with positive new karma. What we sow, we will reap. So, what we do, we will get in return. But, we don't do this with the return in mind. We don't say, "Okay, I see that my partner is overwhelmed with laundry today, so I am going to do the laundry, and then tomorrow, she'd better help me with this." That just doesn't work. We need to do it free of a desired end result in order for it to be pure karmic based.

Another thing we can do in regards to karma, is before you go anywhere, bless the world ahead of you. As you get in the car, bless your car. You bless your travels to your end destination. Before you go into the health club, you send a blessing to the health club, or a blessing to your business, or a blessing to your church. Before you enter your home, you bless your home. Your thoughts are preceding you in blessing the way ahead. This is a very simple exercise to do. A lot of times people forget to do this exercise in the beginning, so you may want to jot yourself a note every day to remind yourself to do it. Before you go anywhere, bless that which is ahead of you.

The next thing we can do in order to become more focused on karma, would be to bless your friends and family every day. The very first thing I do when I get up in the morning is to say a prayer to bless and to relieve all suffering amongst all living beings in this world. Then I go ahead specifically and mention my family, and my friends, and those people I know who are suffering. We are planting powerful karmic seeds by getting outside of ourselves and blessing the world around us. Next, and this is a great challenge, bless those people you do not care for. I am going to repeat this. Bless those people you do not care for. Those people who have hurt you, who have lied to you, or who have been unkind to you. Take moments every day to specifically think of those people and bless them. This is a beautiful karmic seed for you to plant. Also, bless those people who don't care for you. Maybe you don't even know who they are, but just send a general blessing out for all people who speak unkindly of you today, or think unkindly of you today, or who may act unkindly towards you today. Bless them, and allow them to become abundant and happy today. We are planting karmic seeds that will come back and be of such great benefit for us, in the present and in the future. Get focused on your karma. We have so much more control in life than we could ever imagine, if we are actively involved in this concept of planting positive, powerful karmic seeds. You can exceed your own expectations in life when you set yourself up daily with acts of positive karma.

If it seems too difficult to bless people who have hurt you, practice writing in your journal your frustration with those people. Sometimes in order to remove the negative energy we hold within, we must first exorcise those negative emotions on a daily basis. When you become bored writing about how someone has hurt you, you're probably ready to go ahead and contemplate blessing them every day as a way to clean your side of the street.

Is Karma Really an Absolute Law?

But wait, what if our perception of karma is wrong? Sometimes we must challenge long held beliefs to create a new path to create greater focus in our lives.

Think about this. While I love to consider karma as an absolute, it may not be. Now after I explain what I'm talking about, I'd like to leave it up to you to either focus on the old definition of karma, or the new one I'm going to present here.

I want you to feel comfortable with either definition, and remember, the most important belief system is the one that feels best to you, not to society, not to the experts, but you.

Over the past 28 years as a counselor and a life coach, I've worked with some people that did not have the best intentions in life, and my work with them was short-lived. However, even with that said, there are people that go through life taking advantage of others and never really see the repercussions of their actions.

I remember working with a young woman, who actually believed that men were here to serve her needs. She took advantage of men. She would look for men with money, seduce them, get what she needed from them and then walk away. While behind her were people's hearts that were broken, financial lives that were ruined, she skipped ahead without ever thinking about how her actions were hurting others.

I worked with her only for a couple weeks, and when I started to talk to her about her self-centered attitude, her self-centered ways, she would just look at me with this little cute smile and say "David, that's just the way life is. Men are here to take care of women, and I am one of those women that will make sure my needs are met ... And guys who are with me are lucky to be with me."

I did not see any negative ramifications that she saw from treating people incorrectly. And she was hell-bent on keeping her philosophy, her attitude the way it was. She had no desire to change whatsoever. And because she had no desire to change, our work ended pretty quickly.

I also worked with a gentleman who had an affair on his wife, and believed that he was right to have the affair. She wasn't giving him the attention that he wanted sexually. So, he believed, and justified in his own mind, that it was fine for him to go out and to sleep with as many women as he wanted, as long as he kept providing for his wife. He told me he slept perfectly at night, his conscience never bothered him, and his relationship with his wife was quite comfortable.

I had worked with his wife a few times, and of course I could not shatter confidentiality from one client to the next, but she seemed quite happy to have the lifestyle she had, and never brought up the fact that she felt her husband was cheating on her.

To him, which is quite different than a lot of people, there was no need to feel guilty or ashamed of his actions.

Now I give you these two examples, because most people talk about karma, will immediately say that "those two have it coming for them down the road." But do they really? What if their beliefs never change? What if they don't look at any distraction that's going on in their lives as bad?

You see, in this case karma may not be absolute.

I am not encouraging anyone to live in this way, but I'm also going to share a couple other examples that are crucial to think about.

Many times, terrible things happen to great people. I remember working with a young woman who had been brutally raped and left for dead. If you believe in karma, what goes around comes around, then some people would say she had it coming to her.

I worked with this young woman for a year, we helped her to totally turn her life around, and I can tell you in that period of time I never saw any actions in her past that would've justified, karmically, that she deserved to be brutally raped and left for dead.

Or what about a child that was murdered. My good friend, Scarlett Lewis, lost her son Jesse in the Sandyhook elementary school massacre. At six years of age, Jesse could never have done anything in his life to deserve being murdered by a lone gunman in his school.

Now some people who believe karma is absolute, will say that he must've done something in his previous life to deserve this. And I've heard people talk about that too. I'm appalled, I don't buy it, I think many times bad things happen to good people... That has nothing to do with karma whatsoever.

So, think about these examples, and then make up your own mind. This book is meant to have you think deeper. Remember when we talked about affirmations? And I said I thought a great affirmation for someone struggling with alcohol would be "I am an alcoholic, and I need help, and I'm going call this person on this date to get help right now."?

Well you won't find a lot of other books that are going to shoot it straight to you like I am about how to do affirmations realistically. And the same thing with karma. I don't think it's absolute, I think karma can be looked at in many different ways, but let's not take principles like affirmations and karma that you've read in the past, as the golden rule.

As time changes, we should be looking at, and evaluating our deepest beliefs... And asking ourselves if maybe we need to change with the times, instead of staying stuck with the experts and gurus from the past. Something to think about, as you become more focused in life.

Now, dig deep in your soul to create the belief about karma that is best for you. Focus to succeed.

Chapter Review

Stop!

Now that you finished this chapter, it is very important that we slow down, and take a few minutes to answer the questions below.

Writing slows the brain down, and allows thoughts from the subconscious to come into consciousness, and this is one way we will take deep advantage of every chapter in this book.

Write. Right now. Let's keep moving towards our goals, with action steps such as these writing exercises, and not rely on our brain to create the life we desire anymore.

1. What was covered in detail, in this chapter?

_____

_____

_____

2. What was of most interest to you and why?

_____

_____

_____

3. What are 1 or 2 actions steps, relevant to the information in this chapter, that you could take right now to help you to focus more in life? Be specific, and also put the exact day and time that you will take these steps.

_____

_____

_____

Focus! Chapter 8:
The Eight Key Tips to Help You Stay Focused in Life

"You are worthy of every goal you desire."

Here are eight key tips to look at, in order to stay highly focused in life, to assist you in exceeding all of your own expectations.

Number One: I cannot say enough about our morning and evening rituals that we recently went over in this book. There is this incredible opportunity, if you follow those two rituals, to get extremely focused every morning, to start your day off with energy, with opportunity, and then to end your day with gratitude. These two points are so crucial to follow. For those who might be saying, "I don't have time to add anything more to my day," I'd love for you to reconsider. Again, walk into the uncomfortable. Doing those things that we say we "don't have time for" is exactly what the ultra-successful people have been doing in life since the beginning of time. You and I can do the same.

Number Two: Meditation. One of the most powerful ways for us to stay focused in life is through the daily use of meditation. We highly recommend, for those new to meditation, don't try to learn how to meditate via a book. We don't believe for most people that the art of meditation is possible to learn, unless you follow a CD, or if you have the opportunity to join a class. The Buddhists say our mind is like "ten thousand monkeys in a cell." And it is really true. Our minds are wired, especially now, with all of the technology that is bombarding us, from the computer to billboards, to TV, to radio, to satellite radio, and more, with so many thoughts and activities, judgments, and beliefs, that it is almost impossible for the average person to learn how to mediate by themselves. There are great CDs on the market right now that you can purchase to train yourself how to meditate.

If you'd like to get started right now, we have a free meditation video that you can follow, that will only take you moments a day, simply go right here: www.davidessel.com/deepen-your-spiritual-path-now-10-hour-course/.

Meditation is one of the most powerful ways for us to get focused and in alignment with our purpose in life.

Number Three: Yoga or Pilates, or some form of meditative movement. Here we focus the breath; we focus the mind, and we focus the body, all in one activity. These mind- body exercise programs can be incredibly powerful in helping you to focus in life.

Number Four: Exercise. Any type of exercise, including running, walking, aerobic classes, or strength training. If we can bring our mind into the present moment, it will help us to focus. Many people, like myself, who run every week, can get highly focused during their runs. Several segments of this book were created during my regular runs. I have also come up with ideas and concepts for this book during my walks on the treadmill in the gym, which I do every day as well. Exercise flushes the stress-producing chemicals out of the brain, and allows the endorphins to come in to calm, to center, and to focus our attention. Exercise is key on a daily basis in regards to focus in life.

Number Five: Energy work. Energy work can be amazing in helping people to get highly focused in life, whether we are talking about reiki, or acupuncture, massage therapy, or any type of BodyTalk therapy. All of these happen to be techniques that help the mind and body to focus.

Number Six: Prayer. As many of the priests and monks

and nuns have said during my interviews with them, that the goal should be throughout the day to pray without ceasing, to give gratitude for everything that you have throughout the day, and to pray for those in need throughout the day. Prayer helps us become and stay focused as well.

Number Seven: Diet. This might come as a surprise to some people. What we consume can either help us to become focused or stay scattered. First, remove all sugar sources. That means convenient foods that are loaded with sugar. It means, of course, the traditional sugar foods; the snacks, the cookies, the cakes, the candy bars. All of that, yes, remove it. Sugar adds to the hyperactivity in the brain. It also can interfere with our sleep cycles. White flour, remove. White flour is digested by the body just like sugar is. It gives that incredible surge of energy, and then leaves us exhausted. We are trying to move away from all substances that bring us that incredible high and then leave us flat.

Obviously, that is the exact opposite of what we are looking for. Remove all alcohol. Even in the smallest amounts, alcohol clouds the brain. For many people, the next day, even after having something as simple as two glasses of wine, they're not as clear and they're not as focused. Many are allergic to gluten. So, you can find now gluten-free breads and cereals in your grocery stores. Some people are allergic to soy and to milk. Gluten, soy, and milk can actually create "brain fog," just like sugar can, to an individual who is trying to get highly focused in life. It is almost like we are shooting ourselves in the foot if we don't change our diet. We are doing all of this great energy work, this great focus and writing work, we are getting really clear, and then throughout the day we are consuming foods that are working in the exact opposite direction. Next, caffeine. For many people, caffeine is one of those double-edged swords. It offers that instant hit of focus, which is really great; but if caffeine is taken by itself, without any food, we are going to experience the "caffeine crash," similar to what happens after we eat sugar.

Now, what foods can we add to help us get focused in life? First, to keep our blood sugar levels normal, eat every three to five hours. What do we eat during those periods of time? The foods that are best to consume are those that are digested slowly, adding energy to the body over a period of time, versus the rush that comes with simple carbohydrates, white flour, and sugar. That would be nuts, or lean protein sources, as a main component of our daily intake of food. Fruits and vegetables are awesome. We could look for dairy- free foods, for those people who are affected by dairy. Wheat-free foods, for those people who are affected by wheat. Make it simple, "Go back to nature. Eat the simplest, non- processed foods." Another important ingredient, for people who want to stay focused in life, is to consume large amounts of water. For some people, it might be up to ten, fifteen, or even twenty-eight-ounce glasses of water a day to help them stay focused. A wonderful book called "Your Body's Many Cries for Water" explains what happens when we are consuming less water on a daily basis than what we need. It takes away our focus. It increases our fatigue.

Number Eight: Gratitude for what we have right now. I know I mentioned this earlier, but it is so important to say it again. To be grateful for the home, the money, the body, the relationship you have right now, even if it isn't optimal, is a key component of getting focused and moving forward in life. Live in the present moment with gratitude.

Chapter Review

Stop!

Now that you finished this chapter, it is very important that we slow down, and take a few minutes to answer the questions below.

Writing slows the brain down, and allows thoughts from the subconscious to come into consciousness, and this is one way we will take deep advantage of every chapter in this book.

Write. Right now. Let's keep moving towards our goals, with action steps such as these writing exercises, and not rely on our brain to create the life we desire anymore.

1. What was covered in detail, in this chapter?

_____

_____

_____

2. What was of most interest to you and why?

_____

_____

_____

3. What are 1 or 2 actions steps, relevant to the information in this chapter, that you could take right now to help you to focus more in life? Be specific, and also put the exact day and time that you will take these steps.

Focus! Chapter 9:
Why We Shoot for Less Than We Deserve in Life, and What to Do About It

"You are worthy of every goal you desire."

Why do we settle for less than what we desire in life? What gets in our way of staying focused and accomplishing our biggest goals in life? From a mental perspective, it has to do with our belief systems.

First, we have to look at worthiness. Many of us have grown up with, sometimes well- meaning, sometimes not-so-well-meaning parent figures or role models, saying, "We need to be happy with less," or, "We are not worthy of greatness," or, "We are not worthy of great success," or, "The people worthy of great success have PhD's," or, "They come from the other side of the tracks," or, "They...," and the list goes on and on and on. So, the very first thing that blocks us from shooting for what we really want in life is the fact that we don't feel worthy of it. And, that can be changed. Do you know how that is changed? By the daily action steps that we will take to prove we are worthy, even when life isn't working the way that we want it to. And what does that mean? Quite simply, it's this: If your "one thing" is your health, and you know you need to lose weight, in order to feel worthy of a body that you desire, you'd have to get up every day and do the work necessary. We cannot allow excuses to get in the way. We cannot allow rationalizations or justifications to get in the way. For many of my clients over the years, I've seen that all it takes is ninety days. Ninety straight days of getting up and exercising, especially when you don't want to, may be all that is needed to change the belief system that you're not worthy of this massive, beautiful, important goal.

Another reason we shoot for less, is the concept that "it is better to give than receive." I mentioned this earlier in the book. I am repeating it again for a very good reason. Many times, in life, when people are struggling financially, or in love relationships, it is often because of belief systems that say, "It is better that I do for you than do for myself." We see that with a lot of women in marriages with families, or even in marriages without children. They believe that it is better to give than receive, that, "It is better for me to keep doing all of these things to make myself available for my family, my friends, or my church, but not to take the time for me." What happens next? It is called resentment. We start shooting for less than we personally deserve because of the belief that "it is better to give than receive." In reality, it is the best of both worlds, to be able to give and receive, which is what this program is all about.

Why do we shoot for less when it comes to money? Because of those concepts like, "Don't be greedy." "Don't ever make more money than you need." As long as you have enough to get by, be happy with that." Well, that is nonsense. It is not necessary to just be able to scrape by every day. If you desire a great income, you deserve the great income.

We have already setup the process throughout this whole book on how to help you get there.

Sometimes people shoot for less because they have a fear of success. Fear of success means that, "If I lose this weight, I'm going to have to keep working out six days a week for the rest of my life. I don't know if I want to be successful and have to be that accountable." Or with money: "If I make the money I want, that might mean I have to work six days a week to make it. That might mean there are going to be times in my life when I don't take time off, when I don't even take vacations, and I don't know if I want to be that successful and have to be that accountable in life." Do you see what I'm saying? So, sometimes it is the fear of success that is the reason behind us shooting for less than we desire in life. What about the fear of failure? We say, "What would my family think if I went after this huge goal and didn't make it?" "What would my friends think?" "What would my coworkers think?" So, this fear of failure, the fear of being judged by others might be something that holds us back, allowing us to shoot for less in life, and being totally unhappy along the way. We need to shift this. We absolutely need to change this.

Let's do this right now. I want you to write out what your expectations are for every area of your life. Grab a piece of paper, or you can do it right here in this book. I am going to create a whole list for you, with a line next to it for you to write down what your expectations are, and I want you to be specific.

What are your expectations regarding:

- **Money**. How much money do you want to earn on an annual basis? What would make you really, really happy?

_____

_____

_____

_____

_____

_____

- **Your health.** What are your expectations for your body? For your health? How is it that you would like to see it changed?

_____

_____

_____

_____

_____

- **Your love life.** What are your expectations for your love life? How is it that you would like to see altered, if at all?

_____

_____

_____

_____

_____

- **Your relationship with God, or your spiritual path**. How would you like to see this in your life? What are your expectations personally for your own spiritual path? If you don't have any, just leave this blank.

- **Career**. What is it that you would like to see in regards to your own personal expectations for your career path? Where would you like it to go from where it is right now?

_____

_____

_____

_____

_____

_____

Let's Get Big!

Now, in this next section, we are going to go a little higher. We are going to do the same columns, and I am going to ask you to write down next, what it would look like specifically to exceed each of the expectations written above.

As you look at each of these categories of your life, I want you to go big. I want you to write out how you would exceed your expectations in regards to money. This exercise is an example of creating "umbrella goals" that I talked about earlier. The really, really big goals many of us love to go after. Let's say that on the first exercise above, you wrote down that it would be great if you earned seventy-five thousand dollars a year. If you are currently earning forty thousand dollars a year, you might say, "If I could earn almost double it, that would be great."

But, what would it look like specifically for you to exceed the expectations you wrote about above? I mean really exceed it. Would it be $100 hundred thousand? $150 thousand? $200 thousand? What would put you at the brink where you say, "I don't even know if that is possible."

Please don't waste your time here and put a billion dollars a day, or something ridiculous like. Be realistic, but be outrageously excited in your response.

What would it look like to specifically exceed each of your own expectations in life?

- Money:

- Health:

- Love life:

- Relationship with God/Spiritual Path:

- Career:

Next, choose one of those categories, the one that you have denied, delayed, or procrastinated working on, the one that needs the most attention in your life, and the one that if you were to go after would radically change your whole existence. Choose one of those categories, and write it in the line in this book right now.

Now, what specific actions steps do you need to take on a daily basis in order to accomplish this one goal listed above that would exceed your own expectations?

Please write them down right now.

_____

_____

_____

_____

_____

_____

As we continue to move forward in life, I want to go back and review a few really key components in this program of focus.

1. We need to choose one goal at a time, and only one goal at a time.

2. We need to get ready to walk through any resistance or excuses that come up along the way of accomplishing this one goal that will exceed our own expectations.

3. We need to write a daily system to stay focused on, actions steps five days per week.

4. We need to ask to be held accountable by an accountability professional or a partner on a daily basis.

5. We need to clear our mind every morning and see with passion what you want out of life.

6. We need to get or stay involved with courses and books in order to increase our focus on a daily basis. At the end of this book, I will give you a list of a few books that will help you do just that.

Chapter Review

Stop!

Now that you finished this chapter, it is very important that we slow down, and take a few minutes to answer the questions below.

Writing slows the brain down, and allows thoughts from the subconscious to come into consciousness, and this is one way we will take deep advantage of every chapter in this book.

Write. Right now. Let's keep moving towards our goals, with action steps such as these writing exercises, and not rely on our brain to create the life we desire anymore.

1. What was covered in detail, in this chapter?

_____

_____

_____

2. What was of most interest to you and why?

_____

_____

_____

3. What are 1 or 2 actions steps, relevant to the information in this chapter, that you could take right now to help you to focus more in life? Be specific, and also put the exact day and time that you will take these steps.

_____

_____

_____

Focus! Chapter 10:
A Few of the Many People Who Have Helped Me to Stay Focused in Life so that I Can Exceed My Own Expectations

"You are worthy of every goal you desire."

In this chapter, I want to give some credit to just a few of the many people who have helped me to stay highly focused in life to accomplish the things that I have, many of which have exceeded my own expectations. Now, I take credit for the gifts God has given me, and I take credit for the work that I've put in here, but I also must give credit to these people, because for without them, I would not be where I am. And I surely wouldn't have a chance to continue to exceed my own goals and my own expectations in the future without a team of people to help me.

As an introduction to this section, I want to mention that almost everything that I have accomplished in life, and I laugh as I say this, has had very little to do with my academic, intellectual, or scholastic training. In other words, when I look at some of the things that have really blown open my career path, such as hosting national television segments with Fox TV, Lifetime TV, WWOR TV, or hosting nationally syndicated radio shows with Westwood One, and with XM Satellite Radio/Premier Radio networks, all of these have happened because of the people around me who have believed in me, and due to my desire to make a difference in this world. I say this humbly, however, because I have no background, schooling, or education in journalism or in communications, yet much of my career has been based on work in the field of communications. Television and radio entrepreneurs, television and radio hosts, or segment hosts, most of the time are groomed to go into those positions through their academic endeavors. Yet in my case, and there are many people like me around the world, we accomplish things in life because we believe in ourselves and we surround ourselves with people who believe in us as well. If anyone would have asked me years ago, "Do you think that by 2017, that you would have nine books published, two #1 best-sellers, that you would have had the experiences on national television as a host and segment reporter, or you would have, for the past twenty-seven years, hosted national talk radio shows?" I would have said, "Absolutely not." I mean these are examples where I have so far exceeded my own expectations in life because of the help and the belief of others.

Let me run down a list of some of these people and, of course, I am going to leave a lot of individuals out, for which I apologize. If you don't see your name here, know in my heart that I love you. I just wanted to pick out a few people who have had a great impact in my life in regards to focus.

First are my family; my mom and my dad, Pat and Ed Essel, and my sister, Marydiane, and brother, Terry. They have helped me immensely. I would say that one of the greatest things in regards to focus that my family has brought to me is the focus on faith, the focus on God. My family has surrounded me with the absolute love of themselves to me, and also the absolute love of God, as we know God to be. So, I know that my focus and my faith in life have come from my family roots, which are so amazing and so incredible. Through all of my ups, my family has been there, and through all of my incredible challenges, my family has been there. They have helped me to stay focused, on my path to help others.

Maharishi Mahesh Yogi was huge in my life; from the interview that I mentioned in 1996 to today, in helping me to get focused in attacking life, just one major goal at a time.

Joe Cirulli has been a great friend of mine and a mentor since 1986. Joe has helped me focus immensely in so many different arenas, from radically changing my body, as he introduced me to something called the Super Slowdown Training Method, to the concept of being able to do what you love and earn great money at the same time. During one of my greatest trials in life, when I went through a very difficult divorce, he helped me focus. While I was in great pain, Joe helped me focus on the beauty that I brought to this world. He has been immense in my life in regards to focus.

John Biffar, a world acclaimed international film director, has been a friend of mine for over thirty years. John was the producer of my first exercise video, "The Beach Workout." He is an individual who has helped me focus on delivery skills, both on television and on radio. To this very day, John brings an ability to help me focus on my gifts and my talents through his experience in front of the camera. His advice helps me reach people at a deeper level through delivery as well as content. He is a blessing.

Harv Eker, Adam Markel, and Marleen Payne have brought to me, in their own ways, an amazing ability to focus on money. I say that from a very proud perspective, that they have helped me to elevate my awareness and understanding of the way money works, of making money, of saving money, and of spending money as well, in order to have belief systems around money that are extremely grounded and healthy. The focus I have gotten from all three of these people has been incredible.

Caroline Ravelo. Here is a woman who believed in me so deeply that when she opened her publishing company, she came to me and said, "I want your book, 'Heaven On Earth,' to be the first book my company publishes." Caroline, for years now, has been an amazing source of spiritual strength and entrepreneurial strength in my life, and has helped me to stay focused on being able to do both, to be both spiritual and successful as an entrepreneur.

Father Ron at the Hanley Center for addiction recovery is someone who I met when I was in the center to recover from alcoholism. Father Ron came up to me on day three and said, "David, if you surrender to God, if you focus solely on your walk with God, you will never, ever, for the rest of your existence, ever have a craving for alcohol or cocaine again." Father Ron's words were so prophetic that, that evening, I had an immense spiritual awakening, and from that moment forward, regardless of how difficult life has been, his words have rung true. If I surrender, minute by minute, day by day, my life and will to God, I will forever be sober and happy. It is unbelievable, the effect that he had on my life.

Ardith Bissinger has been another person with a huge spiritual effect on my life. I call her one of my spiritual coaches. Without a doubt, she is so grounded in the love of God, that during one of my most difficult experiences, which happened to also be during my divorce, she helped me focus on forgiving myself and my former wife in the middle of my deepest, darkest pain. Without Ardith, during that experience, I would have never understood that you can go into forgiveness at the same moment that you are in deep pain. An incredible experience.

Peggy Solomon, with Westwood One Radio. Peggy helped me when the rest of Westwood One didn't believe that a focused show on health and personal growth could make it in the early nineties on nationally syndicated radio. Peggy was so focused on what I was able to bring to the network and to bring to America's radio airwaves, that she helped build my faith in myself, even when other executives at the network didn't think it would work. Peggy was focused on my gifts and talents to the world, which made our show a huge hit with Westwood One.

Gary Loughlin, my cousin, who has been a real estate mentor, a broker, and an agent for thirty-plus years, in 2000 opened the doorway for me to get into business coaching in the world of real estate by simply giving me a call and saying, "I have a client for you to work with, a new real estate agent. I believe you can help him as he starts his career." When I called back and talked to Gary, I said, "I have worked with people from all different walks of business, but never real estate. Do you think I can actually do it?" His answer was, "Of course you can!" From 2000 to this day, I have worked with hundreds upon hundreds of real estate agents from around the world, helping them to maximize their potential in business. My focus in the world of real estate at one time had me working with seventy agents a week as clients, and it all started with Gary's belief in me and the focus that I could make a difference in that industry.

Richard Gerson was an amazing mentor of mine, who asked me one day in 1984 what I wanted to achieve out of life. When I told him I wanted to be recognized as one of the top health, fitness, and personal growth experts in the world, he looked at me and said, "Then go back to school and get your master's degree." It was those words, and his help to get my master's degree, that opened the doorway for me to be able to create the work and the reputation that I would have never been able to do without furthering my education.

Trevor Oliver, with Premier Radio Network and XM Satellite Radio, had so much faith in me from my work with Westwood One, that he encouraged me to join him at Premier Radio Network and XM Satellite Radio. He wanted me to bring my unique message to the national audience that is deeply needed today: Our need to focus on exceeding expectations, overcoming challenges, and creating the life that everyone desires. This message, backed with Trevor's excitement about my program, brought us back to national syndication. We made a difference in the media landscape, which is often based on sensationalism and negativity, through our positive talk radio show.

Steve Block, one of my earlier mentors, had so much faith in me in business, that he hired me as a spokesperson for his exercise equipment company, SPRI Products. Our focus was based on helping aerobics instructors and personal trainers to maximize their potential in fitness. Steve's faith in me was so great that it opened up doorways to success that I still benefit from today.

Carolyn will always hold a special part in my heart because of her ability to help me focus on my sobriety. A number of years ago, during a conversation we had together, she opened up about her life. At that time we had been dating for several months, and there was something that she needed to talk to me about that was very scary for her to share. It had to do with her sobriety. As she went through the story and told me everything about her life and her work on getting sober, she said she was afraid that when she told me this that it might end our relationship. In other words, I might not want to be with someone who was in recovery. At that time, I was a full-blown alcoholic, a functioning alcoholic, but an alcoholic nonetheless. My evenings consisted, from 8 p.m. on, drinking wine as I completed my work, until I completed enough of the wine itself, where I would fall asleep, better known as passing-out. It was during this incredibly heart wrenching conversation with Carolyn, when my mind was triggered, and my focus finally turned to my sobriety. At the end of this evening, when she had shared such vulnerability and such honesty, without ever asking me to get sober, I went to bed thinking, "This is the time, and this is the message." The next day, waking up, the same thought was in my head: I need to focus on my own recovery, as alcohol was interfering with every area of my life. The very next day, I called and did the intake paperwork over the phone with the Hanley Center for recovery in West Palm Beach, Florida. Without Carolyn's vulnerable, open, and loving communication about her life, I may have never taken the step to save my own. The focus on my recovery has been rewarding ever since, and I owe that to Carolyn.

These are just a few of the many, many people who have helped me to stay focused in the past, in the present, and who will continue to do so in the future. I share these stories with you because, I know that, like the saying goes, "no man is an island," and that if you want to exceed your expectations, you are going to have to surround yourself with people who are doing what you want to do, who are better than you, smarter than you, more inspired than you, and most importantly, who believe in you. Take a moment right now, and as an exercise, write down who has inspired you, who has helped you focus in the past and in the present. Use the lines below just to write down a few of these people.

_____

_____

_____

_____

Next, who do you need to ask to help you today to get to the next level in any and all areas of life, to help you to stay focused on your path of exceeding your own expectations? Write down just a few of the names of these people right now.

_____

_____

_____

_____

_____

_____

_____

_____

The third part of this exercise is to contact the above list. I want you to pick a date and a time that you will e-mail or call this list of people, asking them to help you stay focused and to exceed your own expectations. We will never, ever do this alone; so, let's do it together.

Date and time I will contact these people:

_____

_____

_____

_____

Chapter Review

Stop!

Now that you finished this chapter, it is very important that we slow down, and take a few minutes to answer the questions below.

Writing slows the brain down, and allows thoughts from the subconscious to come into consciousness, and this is one way we will take deep advantage of every chapter in this book.

Write. Right now. Let's keep moving towards our goals, with action steps such as these writing exercises, and not rely on our brain to create the life we desire anymore.

1. What was covered in detail, in this chapter?

_____

_____

_____

2. What was of most interest to you and why?

_____

_____

_____

3. What are 1 or 2 actions steps, relevant to the information in this chapter, that you could take right now to help you to focus more in life? Be specific, and also put the exact day and time that you will take these steps.

Focus! Chapter 11:
Final Thoughts on The Power of Focus

"You are worthy of every goal you desire."

I want to end this book with just a couple of thoughts to prepare ourselves for what is ahead. If we are not prepared, it will be very easy to once again fall off the path of focus and accomplishment, joy, success, and happiness, and back into our old way of living. As we try this new attempt at living a highly focused life, there will be fears that will rise into our mindset. There will be resistance. The resistance will say things like, "This may be good for other people, this concept of focusing on one goal, but I am wonderful as a multitasker. I am going to keep doing what I am doing." Even though it is not giving you the end result you want. These excuses will rise up daily. "I don't have the time or the money to really focus on making money," "to really focus on finding a relationship for my love life," "focus on recovery," or, "to focus on losing weight." The excuses will go on and on and on, and that's why I'm bringing it up right now. I want you to understand that all of this is normal. Saying that I don't have the support system that someone has, or I don't have the education that someone has, are just excuses we use to stay safe and comfortable, even though our safe and comfortable life is not giving us what we want.

Remember back when we talked about canceling negative thoughts? Right now, I want you to revisit that principle, that when doubt comes up, insecurity, jealousy, resentment, anger, rage, or excuses come up, immediately cancel those thoughts. Go back to your focused approach to accomplishing the one major goal in your life that needs your attention right now. As you do this, you will consistently exceed your own expectations.

There is another trap that comes into play that can also

sabotage our success. We might say, "Yeah, I'm struggling financially, but now that I've read this book, and there are other books I can pick up, I'm going to figure this out on my own." Or, "I know that alcohol is not a healthy thing in my life, and it actually might be holding me back in my career or my love life, but I think I'm just going to moderately drink on my own," or, "I'll get sober by myself." The list goes on and on and on. I am going to tell you to stop the thoughts right now. We need our accountability professionals or partners to help us make these major changes. It's easy to fall into the trap of denial by thinking we can make these changes, and accomplish these goals by ourselves. This is an important statement: You have the money you have right now because you've done the best you can by yourself. If you want more money, you need more help. You have the body that you have right now by doing the best you can. If you want a better body, you need more help. You have a relationship with God, or your higher power, that you have right now, by doing the best you can by yourself. If you want a deeper relationship with God or your higher power, you need someone else to help you along the way. I think you get the picture. We need to be held accountable.

I also want you to focus on this book. It is a short book. It is a small book. Reread it every week. Make a decision that for the next thirty days you will read this book once a week. I say this to you openly and honestly, not just because it's my book that I want you to reread, but this principle of rereading the same book for thirty straight days, once a week, has helped me when I'm trying to integrate new changes, philosophies, and education from other authors. Reading it once through is not going to do it. Reading it once a week for four weeks, I promise you, will help you on your path to exceed all of your expectations.

Next, we need to share the message of hope and success with others daily. There is a way to exceed our own expectations in life. Use this book as an opportunity to practice new karma by sharing it with everyone you know. Send this book to your friends; send it to your classmates, your old schoolmates, your co-workers. Send it to people that you don't like. Send it to people that don't like you. In other words, get the message out. Be the bearer of good news. Let people know through your actions that you want them to succeed. Go back and read the chapter on karma. By helping other people, we help ourselves, even if that isn't our sole intention. You can help change the world by spreading this message with every person you can think of. We are blessed to live in the age of the Internet, where you don't have to print this off and put it in an envelope and mail it. A quick, simple click could send the e-book version to everyone in your database. Spread the love, the hope, the freedom, the joy and success that comes from a system that has years of experience behind it, validating its effectiveness.

Huge success is yours, absolutely yours, if you get focused and follow everything that we share with you in this book. It's about going after one goal at a time. It's about grabbing an accountability partner. It's about committing five days a week, a minimum of 90 days of incredible effort to achieve the goals you want in life. Huge success, and I mean huge success, is guaranteed if you do what we share in this book.

Along with all of the success stories we have shared, I can tell you from my own experience of applying these very techniques, my life has radically changed. It was with incredible focus, and committing myself to 365 days in a row of hard work in the area of sobriety, that I shattered a 25+ years addiction to alcohol and drugs.

In one year, I shattered a 30-year addiction to codependency in relationships, where I was afraid to speak openly and honestly with intimate partners. Isn't that amazing? A counselor and life coach who struggled in the world of codependency?

My father, has often commented to my brother, that he is most proud of my sobriety over all of the other huge goals I have accomplished in life. I want the people around you to have the same feeling of pride, after you apply all these principles and come out on the other side a radically changed person. And you can do it. Again, I guarantee it.

Your attitude will change dramatically as well, when you follow the steps that we give you in this book about becoming more focused in life. You will create a powerful attitude. But it won't be because of some fancy affirmation or vision board, those mental techniques will only account for 20% of your success. Your attitude will become more powerful, when you become willing to do the steps on a daily basis you'd rather not do. 80% of your success, huge success in life, will come from your willingness to do what you would rather not do on a daily basis.

As a matter fact when I die, I hope on my gravestone they write "below here lies a man who committed himself to helping others to shatter the illusions and fantastical thinking promoted in the world of personal growth, and rather, gave us a book that helped us radically change our attitudes, through action, action and more action."

As you can imagine, everyone gathers a more powerful attitude when they accomplish huge goals that they have wanted to accomplish for years. So many people I've worked with, outside of myself, when they get clean and sober from alcohol, sugar, nicotine, emotional spending or whatever they're struggling with, feel so much stronger about themselves!

Their confidence improves. Their self-esteem improves. Their attitude improves by doing what we ask you to do in this book, the daily action steps that you would rather not.

Look out, your attitude will go through the roof!

And profound love? I think everyone would love to have a deeper understanding of what profound love really is. And it starts, with us.

Here we go back to action steps gang! When you apply the techniques in this book, and drop the habits that are sabotaging your own physical, emotional, financial goals in life, you are practicing profound self-love.

When you forgive those people from the past two who have stolen from you, lied to you, betrayed you, you are actually doing that to experience more profound self-love.

When you learn how to set boundaries and consequences in relationships, so that people don't walk all over you, or take advantage of you, you are practicing profound love.

And then, when you learn how to communicate with others, forgive others, accept others as they struggle in life, you are practicing profound love.

As I finish this book, I am filled with excitement and energy knowing that if you follow the steps to become more focused, more accountable, more action oriented you will undoubtedly uncover parts of yourself that have been dormant for years.

You will feel invincible. You will feel worthy of love. And you will love yourself at a level you may never have in your life. It will be worth the time, effort, and money spent and the discipline to get to the place you've always wanted to experience, to live in, finally.

Yes, huge success, a powerful attitude, and profound love will be yours. It's coming. Stay focused.

Lastly, if you follow everything that we have written about, you will find in a short period of time that you yourself are worthy of exceeding your own expectations. That you yourself are worthy of a life with a beautiful body, free of addictions, and more money than you need, money that you can share, to give away, to help others with. You can feel worthy of experiencing deep love with a partner, of forgiving those people in the past who have wronged you, as well as forgiving yourself for anything you have done harmful to yourself or anyone else. In other words, the purpose of this book is the purpose of your life. Finding your life's purpose can be done by exceeding our own expectations. As you follow the principles given here, I only have one wish for you: That you will experience life at such a high level, a free level, a level where you are falling deeper in love with yourself every day. You awake every morning and go to sleep every night knowing that the next day brings you one more chance to make a difference in your life, as well as a difference in others' lives. I pray that you will take the seriousness of this message into your heart and soul, and experience what I and thousands of other people have experienced: You are worthy of all you desire.

If I can help you in any way whatsoever, contact me via our websites, www.davidessel.com, www.talkdavid.com. I want what you want for your life, and even more. Have an amazing day.

Chapter Review

Stop!

Now that you finished this chapter, it is very important that we slow down, and take a few minutes to answer the questions below.

Writing slows the brain down, and allows thoughts from the subconscious to come into consciousness, and this is one way we will take deep advantage of every chapter in this book.

Write. Right now. Let's keep moving towards our goals, with action steps such as these writing exercises, and not rely on our brain to create the life we desire anymore.

1. What was covered in detail, in this chapter?

_____

_____

_____

2. What was of most interest to you and why?

_____

_____

_____

3. What are 1 or 2 actions steps, relevant to the information in this chapter, that you could take right now to help you to focus more in life? Be specific, and also put the exact day and time that you will take these steps.

_____

_____

_____

Bonus Gift

Here are the keys to living a focused and successful life – and you can go to my website and download a copy that you can print, frame and hang on the wall: http://davidessel.com/wp-content/uploads/2016/08/DE-Keys-to-successful-life-22.pdf

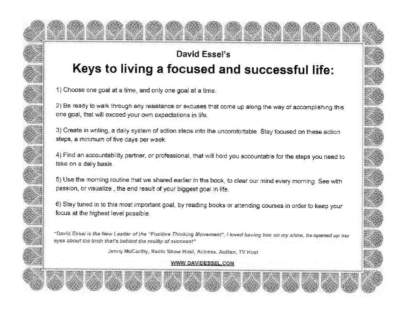

Focus! Appendix 1:

Books to Help You Stay Focused in Life and Exceed Your Own Expectations

The following is a list of books that can help you to maximize your potential, exceed your expectations, and move forward in life at lightning speed.

Remember, there is no need for us to do this on our own. As a matter of fact, if we try to, we will probably end up right where we are today.

- Karmic Management: What Goes Around Comes Around in Your Business and Your Life by Geshe Michael Roach, Lama Christie McNally, and Michael Gordon
- The Diamond Cutter: The Buddha on Managing Your Business and Your Life by Geshe Michael Roach and Lama Christie McNally
- Secrets of the Millionaire Mind: Mastering the Inner Game of Wealth, by T. Harv Eker
- Flow: The Psychology of Optimal Experience, Mihaly Csikszentmihalyi
- The Virgin Diet, JJ Virgin
- Power vs. Force, by David Hawkins
- Practicing the Presence, Joel Goldsmith
- Body for Life, Bill Phillips
- Awakening the Buddha Within, Lama Surya Das
- The Science of Getting Rich, Wallace Wattles
- Feng Shui for Dummies, David Daniel Kennedy

DAVID ESSEL'S COURSES & CERTIFICATIONS

Number one. David offers over 1000 free videos on personal growth at http://youtube.com/superslowdown

Number two. David offers individual one on one courses available for people via Skype, phone or in his office on the following topics:

- Love and relationships
- Codependency kills
- Depression and anxiety
- Financial freedom now
- Holistic addiction recovery
- Public speaking
- Advanced spiritual studies
- Weight loss now and forever
- Sport psychology for athletics
- Life coach certification: level one, level two, level III
- Change your life now!
- Real Estate success
- Life mastery, online course.

All of these courses are available to view at www.davidessel.com/specialty-courses/

Number three. You may also work one-on-one with David as your counselor and life coach on any other topic that you would like assistance with from goalsetting, to procrastination, to finding your purpose in life as well as career change , Grief recovery and more at www.davidessel.com

Other Books by David Essel

Check out these other books by #1 best-selling author,
David Essel

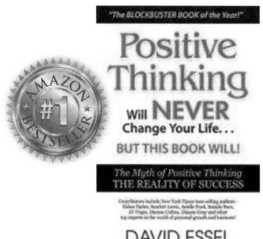

Positive Thinking Will Never Change Your Life But This Book Will: The Myth of Positive Thinking, The Reality of Success

Rock Star:Finding God's Purpose for Your Life

Slow Down – The Fastest Way to Get Everything You Want

God Speaks Through the Heart of a Young Monk

Angel On A Surfboard: Lessons About True Love From a Divine Messenger

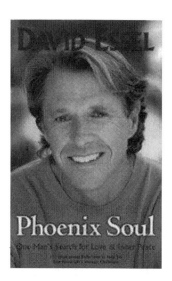

Phoenix Soul: One Man's Search for Love & Inner Peace

How to Maximize Your Potential as a Real Estate Professional

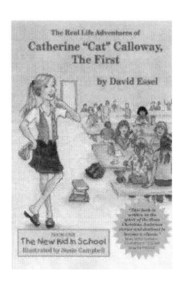

The Real Life Adventures of Catherine "Cat" Calloway, The First

---

Language for the Heart and Soul, Book One: Powerful Writings on Life

---

About the Author, David Essel

David Essel, M. S., *is a number one best-selling author (10), counselor, master life coach, international speaker and radio host whose mission is to positively affect 2 million people or more every day, in every area of life, regardless of their current circumstances.*

Celebrity Jenny McCarthy says "David Essel is the new leader of the positive thinking movement."

*David's work of 38 years is also highly endorsed by the late **Wayne Dyer**, "Chicken Soup for the Soul" author **Mark Victor Hansen**, as well as many other celebrities and radio and television networks from around the world.*

*He is verified through **Psychology Today** as one of the top Counselors and Life Coaches in the USA, and is a "Verified Relationship Expert" through **Marriage.com**.*

Professional Speaker

Bring David in to your business, corporation or non-profit organization, and receive up to 50 of his book, "Focus!" absolutely free.

David gave the commencement address recently at the Syracuse University graduation ceremony, and has spoken to corporations like Nestle and Discover Card, as well as non-profits such as the March of Dimes.

For information, visit: www.DavidEssel.com/speaker